A NARRATIVE

OF THE

EARLY LIFE, TRAVELS, AND GOSPEL LABORS

OF

JESSE KERSEY,

LATE OF

CHESTER COUNTY, PENNSYLVANIA.

PHILADELPHIA:
T. ELLWOOD CHAPMAN,
No. 1 South Fifth Street.
1851.

STEREOTYPED BY
S. DOUGLAS WYETH, AGT.
No. 7, Pear Street, Philad'a.

Printed by DEACON & PETERSON.

CONTENTS.

INTRODUCTION.

TESTIMONY CONCERNING JESSE KERSEY, AN APPROVED MINISTER IN THE SOCIETY OF FRIENDS.

THE undersigned, members of the Western Quarterly Meeting, being drawn together from a concern that some of the weighty expressions of our beloved friend, in his last sickness, together with a few of the important particulars of his eventful life, might be preserved, in connection with his writings, feel an engagement to give forth the following.

He was the son of William and Hannah Kersey, of Yorktown, Pennsylvania. Was born on the 5th of 8th month, 1768. In his childhood and early youth, he was much exposed to the corrupting influence of vain and vicious company; but through the guardian care and religious concern of his parents, and the restraining influence of the Divine gift in himself, he was preserved in a great degree from the contamination of guilty compliance with the customs and manners of the time, by which he was surrounded. In a manuscript found among his papers, he says of himself: "I have frequently looked back with gratitude and wonder, that I should have wholly escaped the crime of using profane language, notwithstanding it was common among my play-fellows. This preservation, I am aware, was without any merit in me, still I cannot reflect on it without a real satisfaction; and I fully believe that those who have children under their care, cannot be too watchful in keeping them from that hardihood of mind and manners, which is always attendant, when an early habit of using wicked words, is allowed or acquired." It appears that among the first temptations that beset him to disobey his parents, was to accept the invitations of his youthful companions, to wander about with them on the first day of the week; and although he was at a loss to imagine why he should be restrained from this, yet he says, "in every instance, such indulgence rendered him very unhappy afterwards." It seems that on looking back upon the scene of his juvenile sports and pastimes, he was ready to believe that the regrets he had felt for having disobeyed his parents, might have been occasioned more by his affection for them, than from any clear conviction, at the time, of the evil of the practice.

Among the influences that operated to restrain him, he mentions, that "his mother's tears were not soon forgotten." About the fourteenth year of his age, he had frequent convictions for his follies, which induced him often to think it was necessary to be more guarded. Yet he continued to join with his acquaintances in their diversions, until at length those feelings of conviction seemed to be much worn off, and his taste for cheerful company to have left but little relish for serious things. "My parents," he continues, "carefully kept me to meetings, and the frequent reading of the Scriptures." "In meeting I would sometimes feel sensible that my folly and loose state of mind were condemnable; but more frequently, after being among my giddy companions, condemnations would attend me, when my head was laid on my pillow."—In his sixteenth year, he was placed as an apprentice in the city of Philadelphia; on leaving the paternal roof, he comforted himself with the thought, that being removed from his old acquaintances, and now likely to form new ones, he could seek such as were "more serious and circumspect," and in his moments of retirement, he became impressed with the belief, that "to be happy he must be more thoughtful and serious." In his new situation, however, he had his trials and temptations, but in the companionship of his fellow apprentices, who were "habitually profane," the first thing that he attempted, was to promote a reformation among them; and although his efforts seemed, at first, to make some impression, yet soon afterward they subjected him to ridicule.

However, when it became apparent to them, that he "was serious and settled" in his course, his remarks with regard to their profanity, were received very differently by his shop-mates, and at length he had the "satisfaction to see this evil practice wholly broken up, and a gradual improvement in other respects." When about the age of seventeen he appeared in public as a minister, having sometime previously received a clear impression, that his duty in life, was not to be confined to a private sphere; and having submitted to the call, "the serene and quiet state" that he experienced upon taking his seat, after his first appearance, was to his mind "conclusive evidence" that he "had not mistaken" his duty. "In the exercise of his gift," he observes, "I felt many fears, arising from a consideration of the solemnity of the work; but as I kept humbly attentive to the Divine impressions, I found His grace was all-sufficient." And speaking from his after experience, he adds, "I have been convinced that much depends upon wholly relying on the all-sufficiency of Him, who promised to be to his servants, mouth and wisdom, tongue and utterance."

In the year 1789, having completed his apprenticeship, he left Philadelphia, and opened a school in Chester County, and the year following, was united in marriage with Elizabeth, the daughter of Moses Coates, a connection which he regarded as a great blessing to him. And having removed to the place of his nativity, he began the requisite preparations for carrying on his trade. With a mind deeply devoted to the advancement of the Redeemer's kingdom among men, and in view of the dangers attending worldly pursuits, he says in his narrative, "I had many fears, lest after all I had known of the mercy and goodness of a Gracious Father and Almighty Friend, I might fall into weakness and entanglements." It seems he did not succeed in business at York, and upon deliberate consideration and consultation with his friends, he removed again to East Caln in Chester County. He had many trials tending to discouragement, in reference to which he remarks, that "under all circumstances, my confidence was maintained in the care of Divine Providence over me. I believed, in the promise, that they who seek first the kingdom of God and His righteousness, shall have all things necessary added unto them, and at times in our religious meetings, I felt sensible that I was not forsaken. My mind was tendered under the assurances of Divine love to man, and in these seasons I could discover, that it was all in Wisdom that I was tried." Soon after his settlement at East Caln, he felt himself called on a religious visit from home. In the course of this journey he observes, "my confidence in the safety of submitting to the clear openings of duty, was in no degree lessened." The difficulties he had to encounter, in providing for his family, and being of a delicate constitution, inclined him to relinquish the business he followed, and he again commenced teaching school; while employed therein, he felt an engagement to pay a religious visit to several of the Southern states. The prospect, he remarks, "was serious in every view that I could take of it; I had now two children to provide for, and still remained poor." In this visit he spent three months time and travelled about seventeen hundred miles.

Still labouring under difficulties and embarrassments, he was at times almost ready to sink under discouragement. But, to use his own words, "having been favoured to rise above these doubts and fears, which had almost destroyed my confidence in the particular Providence of the Almighty, my heart became enlarged as at other times, in love to all mankind, and melted into tenderness under a sense of the Love of God. Now prospects of journeys and engagements for the promotion of righteousness opened before me." About the year 1804, he visited England and Ireland; and was afterwards extensively engaged in the ministry within this and other Yearly Meetings; and in the year 1814, again visited the South under a concern, in especial relation to the cruel and unrighteous system of American Slavery, and the mode of deliverance from its terrible consequences, having opportunities with the President of the United States, and other distinguished men, and holding meetings among the people of color and others. On his return, it appears his mind was comforted in the belief, that way would yet be made safely to remove what he describes as "one of the greatest evils that ever the *Spirit* of *delusions* has succeeded in imposing upon mankind."

As a Minister, he was remarkably qualified to enlist the attention of his hearers, to fix their minds upon the glorious and sublime truths of the Christian religion, and often was he followed and admired by crowds of gratified auditors not of his own persuasion. In the morning of his promise, and the meridian of his day of usefulness, his society was courted by the wise and the learned,—his affability of manners,—his grave and dignified deportment,—the soundness of his principles,—the beauty and simplicity of his style of address,—heightened in their effect by the depth of his devotional feelings, gave an interest and a charm which gained him many admirers. And it may be, that the caresses of an admiring multitude, are more potent for evil influence upon their object, than the heavy pressure of adverse fortune,—that the voice of flattery is more dangerous to the safety of its recipient, than the coldness of neglect, or the stern language of rebuke;—certain it is, that, "to err is human," and the subject of this memorial was not exempt from human frailty. But although the extremes of opposite causes, operating upon a peculiar temperament, may in their ultimate effects, have weakened his capacity for usefulness, and eclipsed the brightness of his renown;—though the history of a portion of his life, notwithstanding his extraordinary endowments, may afford melancholy evidence of the danger of the practice, which was generally prevalent in society at that time, of using intoxicating liquors as a beverage,* yet we doubt not, the arm of preservation was still underneath, and that by Divine aid, and the instrumentality of his friends, he was favoured measurably to maintain the conflict in that state and condition of mind, in which he could have adopted the language, "*His compassions fail not, they are new every morning.*"

In his common intercourse among men he was uniformly guarded in his expressions, and some useful lesson of instruction was ordinarily blended in his discourse,—it has been said of him that he was a man that never talked nonsense,—if he was cheerful, it was without the accompaniment of lightness or levity. There was a dignity and nobleness about him that commanded respect, and gave evidence of an exalted aim; and it was his consolation in the evening of life, to believe, that amidst all his weakness and trials, and his afflictions, of which he had many, he had never

* In justice to the subject of this memoir the reader should also be informed that he was in earlier life afflicted with a troublesome and dangerous disease, for the relief of which, and by the advice of his medical attendant, he was led into the use of opium. Thus a habit was unconsciously formed, the force of which can be best appreciated by those who have themselves long indulged in the use of some narcotic or stimulating article. The combined effects of this habit and of pre-existing disease unhappily so undermined and weakened the nervous system as to render his ulterior existence very uncomfortable, unless sustained by opium or some other stimulant—and created a seeming necessity for their frequent use.

been wholly forsaken by the beneficent author of his being, in whom he trusted.

On the conclusion of a religious visit of considerable extent, performed in the year 1835, reflecting upon the ability which had been furnished him beyond any former experience, and the sympathy and unity of Friends, of which he had never before known a greater manifestation, he felt, as he expresses it, cause to say, "return oh my soul to the place of thy rest, for the Lord hath dealt bountifully with thee."

He was a member of Kennet Monthly Meeting for a short time previous to his death, during which period he made some visits abroad, though in declining health, and so late as the year 1845 obtained a minute to attend the Yearly Meeting of New York, where notwithstanding his great bodily infirmity, he was present at all its sittings. It has been observed that the power of Truth had accompanied his several communications, in so remarkable a degree, that the meeting, near its conclusion, contrary to its accustomed order, and the caution by him delivered against a departure from its previous practice, directed an endorsement of his minute, expressive of unity with him, in his gospel labours: after which he appeared in supplication,—when under a solemn covering, the meeting closed.

In the fall of the same year he proceeded under a concern to visit the families of Friends throughout the several branches of the Monthly Meeting of which he was a member the only visit of the kind he was ever engaged in. His strength failing him, before its completion he retired to his home, and on the 18th of the 10th month was taken to his bed. During his confinement no murmur or complaint was observed to escape his lips, but often was he heard to say he had "no pain" and that he believed "it was the will of his good Master to give him an easy passage." To a friend who had been speaking of the great change that had taken place within his time, in regard to the use of intoxicating drinks, he stated among other things, that he was rejoiced at the reformation that had been made in the society of Friends in that particular. A few days before his death he said there was nothing in his way, "not a cloud nor the shadow of a cloud" resting on his mind. At another time—"I feel that my course is nearly finished, and I am ready to be offered up." To a friend who called to see him, he said, "Thou canst witness with what composure and sweet contentment a servant of God can die." To another—"I am very poorly, and believe my end is near, give my love to my friends, tell them that I don't know that I ever felt more for them, but my bodily powers are fast declining." On the 24th two friends being introduced and inquiring how he felt, he answered, "I am here yet, but am wearing away—growing weaker every hour—I have not been able to converse much, my powers of speech are so wasted,—but I love the company of my friends,—and I love it in the spiritual life that needs no words." Then after a little pause, he spoke of his concern to serve his gracious Master through the course of a long life which was now near its close. Of his unshaken faith in the teachings of the heavenly principle of Light and Life in the soul, and of the prospect before him of a blessed immortality; saying, in humble confidence,—"I have fought the good fight, I have kept the faith,—and now have the consoling evidence, that there is laid up for me a Crown, which God, the righteous Judge, will give in his own time." Then looking round on those in the room with a benignant smile upon his countenance, he expressed the hope that they would be encouraged "to walk by the same rule and to mind the same thing."

After which his strength failed fast, and on the morning of the 26th he passed quietly away, being in the 78th year of his age.

His remains were interred on the 28th at West Chester, in Friends' burying ground in the presence of a large assemblage of Friends and others.

Signed 3d Month 12th, 1850.

George Martin,	Solomon Pusey,
Thomas Jenkinson,	Richard M. Barnard,
Joseph Chandler,	Joseph S. Walton,
John Chandler,	Ezra Michener,
Benjamin Swayne,	Wm. E. Bailey,
David Walton,	Amos Barnard,
Amy Pennock,	Edith Jenkinson,
Ruth Pyle,	Maria Jane Chandler,
Sarah Bailey,	Abigail Walton,

Ann Chandler.

JESSE KERSEY, ON THE DEATH OF HIS WIFE.

Ah! whither, sainted spirit, art thou gone,
And left thy tender spouse now all alone?
Our time together sweetly passed away,
While we were partners, each returning day.
But now, my love, no more can I behold
Those brilliant eyes that oft thy kindness told.
No; dearest partner,—thy blest race is run,
And thou art told that all thy work is done.
While we were passing through this world of care,
How oft thy counsel bid me not despair.
When storms and tempests seem'd on ev'ry side,
In thee I found (however greatly tried)
A mind superior to the darkest hour,
Whose trust was firm in the Almighty's power.
Thy gentle spirit, govern'd by the Truth,
Maintain'd with constancy the vows of youth.
Nor did thy soul e'er separated stand
From thy all-wise Creator's blest command.
But, being faithful to "the *Light within*,"
Was thereby kept from each besetting sin.
And having known a heart that was sincere,
Thy end was peace,—thy future prospects clear.
Thus pass'd the partner of my life away,
The blessed subject of eternal day.
No sorrows, griefs, nor clouds of dark despair,
But joy and peace forever centre there.
Oh! may her offspring, guided as she was,
By principles Divine, and holy laws,
Enjoy with her the pure reward of peace,
Nor from the beauty of her life e'er cease.
Then will they ever prove themselves to be
Examples from all vice and folly free.
Thus wisely meeting ev'ry task assign'd,
In ev'ry trial they will be resign'd.
And when their race on earth shall have an end,
Jehovah God will be their lasting Friend.

JOURNAL.

CHAPTER I.

Containing an account of his early life, up to his sixteenth year.

My parents' names were William and Hannah Kersey, and I was born in Yorktown, Pennsylvania, on the 5th day of the 8th month in the year 1768. Growing up in a considerable town, I early had an opportunity of mixing in company of various kinds. But by the watchful care of my parents I was preserved out of some of the evils that were common among the children of the place. My fondness for diversion increased with my years; and at an early period I felt inclinations to seek entertainment from sports that were forbidden by my parents,—to whose watchful care over me I am indebted, under Providence, for preservation from many evils common to youthful years.

I have frequently looked back with gratitude and wonder, that I should have wholly escaped the crime of using profane language,—notwithstanding it was common among my play-fellows. This preservation, I am aware, was without any merit in me. Still I cannot reflect on it without a real satisfaction; and I fully believe, that those who have children under their care, cannot be too watchful in keeping them from that hardihood of mind and manners which is always attendant when an early habit of using wicked words is allowed or acquired.

Among the first circumstances which I recollect, that gave me dissatisfaction, was the prohibition of my parents against wandering about on the first day of the week. I could not imagine why they denied me a practice which was general. My acquaintance would often call for me on that day, and seem disappointed when they found I could not go with them. At some few times, I stole away and mixed with them through the afternoon: but in every instance such indulgence rendered me very unhappy afterwards.

By an early and proper attention to this subject, children and young people might be induced to prefer spending the afternoon of first day in reading and quietness: and the heads of families being separated from their worldly concerns,—would find a pleasing entertainment in mingling with the children, and giving them useful information. If we were to combine with these opportunities of private family improvement, the frequent reading of the Scriptures, it might very much tend to fix an early attachment to their valuable contents. On this subject, the example and practice of the parents of John Woolman, are worthy of consideration.

In one instance of my wandering from home on first day afternoon, I was followed by my mother,—who found me on the commons amongst a number of boys. I well recollect, that the instant I saw her my mind was filled with shame and confusion; and in this state I followed her home. She made no remarks to me on the way, except putting the question to me, "How could thee do so?" My heart was filled with sorrow, so that I could make no reply. When we got home, and sat down, I noticed the tears rolling down her cheeks. This made a very deep impression upon me, and I desired her not to be grieved about me; promising I would not do so any more.

But I have since thought that those impressions and feelings resulted more from the affection I felt for her, than from any clear conviction which I then had of the evil of the practice. I cannot, however, look back to the circumstance without also remembering, that my mother's tears were not soon forgotten; nor could I think, for a considerable time afterward, of attempting to commit the same kind of trespass upon her feelings. Still the love of play, and frequent opportunities of company during my waking hours,—often drew me into sports and amusements, and particularly into company which was objectionable to my parents. As they checked and reasoned with me, I would frequently think that their restrictions were hard to bear, and would therefore trespass their orders; in doing which, sometimes they would detect me,—and at others, I would escape.

In one instance, I had an irresistible choice to go to a horse-race; about which I knew it would be in vain to consult my parents, and therefore stole away without their knowledge. The races were what were called "the four-mile heats." I recollect, that when the poor animals had run what was called "the first heat," I felt sorry to see them panting for breath, and wet with sweat; and some thoughts on the subject of a serious character were presented to my mind: but I found the longer I stayed, the more I was entertained with the scene. After the first and principal races were run, there were several others: and in one instance I was asked to ride. At first I felt some ambition to undertake it;—but suddenly a thought struck me, that if my parents knew that I had rode, it would grieve them; and I was favored with firmness sufficient to resist the temptation. But when I was asked why I would not ride,—it seemed to try me considerably. The answer I gave was, that I should offend my parents if I did. And having got clear of them, I soon went home, where my anxious parents were glad to see me. They inquired whether I had been to see the races? To which I gave them an honest answer, and hoped they would excuse me, as I did not think I should ever wish to go again. I also told them how I had managed an application which was made to me to ride, and the answer I had given why I would not do it. With my conduct in that case, they were satisfied. After commending my firmness, and making some remarks upon the evil tendency of horse-racing, they hoped I would never wish to see another.

My age at this time I do not recollect; but I never after went to see another horse-race. Whatever may be said in defence of this evil, I believe it is associated with cruelty,—that it generates a love of gambling,—and that the crowds of loose and disorderly people who assemble on those occasions, are very unfit company for innocent young persons to be exposed to,—and that among the professors of Christianity, it cannot be countenanced, without departing from the purity of the principles inculcated by Jesus Christ.

It was customary in the town of York, for apprentice lads and others, frequently to be in the streets in companies after dark; but my parents would not permit me to be with them. This restriction I often thought a hard case; and sometimes I would get out without their knowledge. This gave me an opportunity to notice, that there was more bad language and fighting under the cover of night, than was common in the day. And I now believe that the morals of many boys who are permitted to run the streets at night, have been much injured by it; and that they prompt one another to many evils which they would be both afraid and ashamed to commit in open day.

It would no doubt be much better, if those who have the charge of children were more attentive to this point. By a little care, they might be introduced to the practice of spending the evenings in the improvement of their learning: and as they become interested in their studies and in reading, they would become satisfied at home. I have often regretted that so much liberty is given to the youth,—particularly to bound children in our cities, and that they are so much neglected by those who have the care of them. The quarreling and tumult among them, so common under cover of the night, is conclusive evidence that many who have the charge of boys, care very little about them, more than to see that they perform their portion of labor; and when this is accomplished, they may run at large, and do as they please.

About the fourteenth year of my age, I frequently had convictions for my follies, which induced me often to think it was necessary to be more watchful and guarded in my conduct; and sometimes I would resolve to quit the sports in which I had indulged. But when fresh temptations presented, I was soon led away.—Again I would resolve to be more firm, and act the part which should keep my mind easy. But month after month passed away, and instead of making any valuable stand, I continued to join with my acquaintances in their various diversions;—until, at length, those feelings of conviction seemed to be much worn off.

My father's house was frequently resorted to by Friends. But their manners were so different from what I observed among the gay people of the place, that I could not think it desirable to grow up a Friend. I imagined that there must be an error in the habits and ideas of a people who seemed to me to have scarcely any cheerfulness about them. I observed that some of our visiters differed from others. They were not all equally gloomy. A degree of sociability and pleasantry was practised by some, whilst others seemed to me to be almost under the dominion of melancholy. Among our visiters, there were some instances of men who differed from the Society of Friends in our parts generally. Their hats were white, and their clothes of the natural color. It was not easy for me at that time, to account for such singularity. If my parents, or Friends of the town, had given no extraordinary attention to these men, I believed I should have taken little notice of the circumstance. But as those persons seemed to me to be held in higher estimation, I was ready to suppose that in order to become the complete Friend, and pass among strangers as such,—if I grew up a member of the Society, I must get the white hat, and adopt this general singularity of appearance.

The impression upon my mind, which arose from those cases of singularity, was, about this time, very unfavorable to Friends, as a religious Society. I would reflect on the liberty other boys had, and upon the gay and cheerful conduct of their parents. I would contrast this with the restrictions I was under, and with the gloomy manners of Friends; and frequently thought to myself that I never would be like them.* One thing however, I could not avoid noticing, and that was, the conduct and conversation of Friends were innocent. I heard no swearing or rough language in their company. But among the other inhabitants of the town, I frequently heard bad language. They called their children rough names. This I could not approve of.

By contrasting the mild language of the Society with the language of other people, I believe it will be seen that the youthful mind, among the former, will be kept much more free from the moral taint, almost inseparable from those who are daily within hearing of the profane language of the latter.

By degrees, my taste for cheerful company had so fully worn off the love of serious subjects, that I could have little relish for either books or society, that were serious. Still, my parents kept me carefully to meetings, and frequently in the afternoons of first days, to reading the Scriptures. In meetings, I would sometimes feel sensible that my folly and loose state of mind, were condemnable: but more frequently, after being among my giddy companions, condemnation would attend me when my head was laid on my pillow.

Thus the time passed on, without my gaining any firm stand against that lightness and folly to which I was prone. At length, it became necessary for me to

*It is believed that this reference was made to a company of young men who undertook to imitate John Woolman in their manner of dress. They thus rendered themselves conspicuous for a time, and were esteemed sincere. But, "not having root in themselves," they became formal, and their zeal for external appearance soon "withered away."

leave my parents, in order to learn a trade. In this prospect, I comforted myself with the idea that I should probably be removed from my old acquaintances; and that, in forming new ones, I would look out for those who were more serious and circumspect, than the companions I should leave. The impressions made on my mind in moments of retirement, that if I expected to be happy, it was necessary for me to be more thoughtful and serious, I now flattered myself could be attended to without the difficulty of making the change in the midst of my present associates, and without becoming the subject of their ridicule.

CHAPTER II.

A review and narrative of his apprenticeship, and account of his appearance in the ministry, with remarks.

In the preceding part of my history, I have given some account of the amusements and course of my early life, and of the fondness that I had for youthful pleasures. I shall now attempt to retrace the scenes through which I passed during an apprenticeship of five years and three months in the city of Philadelphia.

In the spring of the year 1784, being in the sixteenth year of my age, I left the care and protection of my parents, and went to live among strangers. The man I was placed with, was a potter by trade, and a member of the Society of Friends. On my introduction to him and his wife, I was favorably impressed toward them both. They appeared to take me into their family with a concern for my welfare. They informed me that the boys they had, did not behave as well as they could wish, and they hoped I would be careful not to follow any of their bad practices;—they also expressed a hope that I would spend my leisure hours in the house with them. Those professions of kindness and concern, I considered as evidences of their interest in my welfare, and of their good-will towards me.

But I soon found my situation very different from that experienced in my father's house. There, I was on an equality with every member of the family; but here, the family was divided into several classes. No unity or friendship appeared to prevail, but division, discord, and envy. The apprentice-boys had no apparent attachment to the family, or the heads of it; nor had *they* much (if any) for the boys.

Under such circumstances, it is easy to see that difficulties were to be met with. If I chose the society of the family, I was to be rejected by my shop-mates. If I made the latter my uniform company, I was liable to all the charges of misconduct that might fall upon them. In this critical and delicate situation, a circumstance occurred which soon settled the question. The next day after my entrance into the family, I found my station was different from any condition I had ever been placed in before. The master, his wife, and their children, were in the habit of sitting down to one table,—and the boys to another. The remains of the provision on which the master, his wife and children had dined, were placed on the boys' table; and the breakfast and supper were also taken in the same separate manner. In short, there were two tables kept morning, noon, and night. I concluded that if my station could not be with the heads of the family at meals—and that if, because I was their apprentice, I must be placed below their children, I was not fit to be a part of the parlor company.

From such considerations, I made up my mind to be as distant as the order of the house appeared to place me. There was a kind of resentment excited in me, by the degradation that I thought I was placed under. I considered my father's family as respectable as the family in which I now was; and why so great a difference was made between me and the children of my master, I could not conceive. Had the separation been only when they had company, I could easily have apologized for it: but finding it uniform, on all days of the week alike, company or no company, it produced in my inexperienced mind, a settled aversion to the family.

My motive for being particular in relation to the foregoing system, is not with any view to implicate the family as being singular in their practice from many other Friends engaged in mechanical or mercantile pursuits; but to show how prejudicial it was to me and my fellow-apprentices, and the unfavorable impressions it made towards the family. Nor have I any doubt, that as a general rule, it would be much better for the master of every family to sit at the head of his table, and preserve proper order.

The discontent with the provisions, when they were good enough, and the disrespect and prejudice which may be generally expected where two tables are thus kept—can scarcely be conceived by any who have not had an opportunity fully to experience it.

Having now become the companion of the boys, the first thing that I thought necessary, was to attempt promoting a reform among them. They were habitually profane; and I could not think of descending into this corrupt practice. I therefore informed them, that I was disappointed in finding them so addicted to the use of bad language,—and that I had expected in the work-shop of a Friend, no such practice had ever existed. At the moment, these remarks seemed to make some impression on my shop-mates: but this soon subsided, and I was answered with ridicule.

I now recollected my prospect in favor of becoming more serious under the advantage of leaving my old acquaintances behind when I became an apprentice. It was evident, that if I abode by my resolution among my new companions,—the ridicule which I had dreaded, would be to be endured under circumstances still more trying. In the former case, I could retire out of the way of company that was unpleasant: but in my present case, I was confined to the same room, and could not avoid my shop-mates. I could therefore see but little encouragement to attempt a change toward a more serious life. It seemed as though all things conspired to convince me, that unless I conformed to the manners and habits of my fellow-apprentices,—any difference in my conduct would subject me to their abuse. This I dreaded,—and apprehended I could not endure. I had many serious thoughts about what was best for me to do. Sometimes I would almost make up my mind to return to my parents, and state to them the reasons why I could not stay. At other times I would suppose it might be possible to steer a kind of middle course; that is, not to go into the extremes in which the boys indulged,—nor wholly to withdraw from them. On one point, however, I became fully settled, and that was, that I would not embrace their profane language;—but in every other respect be their companion.

Accordingly, I set out on this plan. I wandered

about with them at nights; and on my return home, felt miserable. Sometimes the thought would occur to me, that if I respected my parents as I ought to do, I would not so soon depart from their restrictions and advice; but would as regularly stay at home after dark, now I was separated from them, as I did when living with them. But those compunctions would be silenced by considering that the case was now altered, —that I had not the same associates as formerly,—and that if I were to stay at home with the family, I should soon have the ill-will of the boys. Thus I reasoned and persuaded myself that my practice was not from disrespect to my parents, but rather the result of untoward circumstances. With such like reasonings, I endeavored to silence those convictions that frequently distressed me when out at nights. But they all proved a vain refuge; and trouble succeeded trouble. In the house I had no comfort:—in the shop, all seemed disorder;—in the street, all was confusion. Friends (in the city) I seemed to have none.

Under these circumstances, day after day, I was unhappy; and that unhappiness was increased by occasionally joining with the boys in their mischievous acts toward the family. At length, I had so fully plunged with them into folly and wantonness, that I saw the attachment of my master and mistress was not towards me in the degree that appeared in the beginning of my apprenticeship.

When my feelings of distress were almost insupportable, I went with one of my shop-mates to attend a sale of books. He told me the place was pleasant and entertaining. When we arrived at the book store, we found it shut. My companion said, the auctioneer was a play-actor, and that he must be gone to the play. I was now for turning back; but he urged me to go on, and said we should be home time enough. I consented, and we went on. But I had no sooner got in sight of the play-house, than I was astonished at the terrible tumult which surrounded it. Those who were without, with clubs and stones were swearing and threatening to break their way into the house;—while those within were threatening vengeance on them if they did not desist. During the few minutes that I stood looking on, I thought that if ever a spot upon the earth was sufficiently vicious and wicked for the ground to give away under it, and swallow up the company, this was so; and I felt afraid to trust myself near. But my shop-mate rushed into the throng, and I left him. After looking on the dreadful scene a few minutes, I went solitarily along the streets home.

This evening's ramble wound up my wanderings at night with my fellow apprentices. The powerful convictions and condemnation that I felt on my way from the play-house home,—were not forgotten for many days. By this time, I had also so entirely lost the friendship of the family, that I saw I had no place in their sympathy or affections. The degree of serious thoughtfulness which had taken place in my mind did not pass without being noticed by the boys: they also observed that I excused myself from going with them as at other times. A suspicion commenced with them that I was endeavoring to get into favor in the house. They grew jealous of me, and sometimes showed a degree of ill-nature toward me. My situation daily became more and more unpleasant, until I was brought to the necessity of plainly telling them, that for the future I should not join in any thing that tended to wound the peace of my own mind.

The effect of this testimony was soon felt. I was rejected by the boys and treated with ridicule. In the house I had no friends, and in the shop all seemed sour and uncomfortable. Under these circumstances, my only comfort was in being alone. In this neglected and tried condition, I passed several months before any relief was provided for me. Under these solitary and discouraging feelings, our religious meetings became very desirable to me: and in order to get to them, I would rise early on meeting day, and get my work so forward that no objection could be made to my going. And when at meetings, my concern was simply for preservation, and that I might have firmness and patience sufficient to endure without murmuring, all the trials that might come upon me;—fully believing that they were permitted in order for my refinement.

Sometimes in these solemn opportunities, when musing on the situation in which I was placed, my mind would be led back to the opposition I had often made to the Light within; and I would feel a degree of resignation to suffer, as an atonement for my many offences.

The diligence that was manifest in my attandance of religious meetings, and the serious manner in which I sat in them, did not go unnoticed. Several young men of circumspect and exemplary conduct, had been turning their attention toward me; and after the close of one of our evening meetings, two of these, Charles Williams and Michael Monier, very kindly spoke to me, and said they were glad to see my diligence in attending our meetings. These young men continued to be my kind and useful companions, during the remainder of my apprenticeship and residence in the city. Very soon after this first interview, Charles invited me to his father's house, and the whole family gave me a generous welcome the first time I visited them. I now had a Friend's house to retire to in the evenings, where I could spend the time profitably with a judicious and prudent companion, whom it was safe to inform of my difficulties, and consult when I thought necessary. Our attachment to each other increased from time to time, and continued without any interruption during the life of Charles Williams; and in his death I felt the loss of a firm and valuable friend.

This happy commencement of new and profitable acquaintances had a great tendency to encourage me to maintain with firmness my integrity to the pointings of Truth. I now saw that if my situation was unpleasant through the day, I could in the evening have useful and agreeable company. I believed too, that it was a mark of providential care over me, thus to open my way into such society. Under these ideas, I began to hope that my past follies would be forgiven. For, although I had felt much of the weight of condemnation, and had endeavored to be on my guard against increasing the occasions of it,—yet I had no satisfactory evidence that my transgressions were forgiven. When I heard others speak of the consolations they enjoyed, and particularly of their confidence that if they maintained their steadfastness for the time to come,—the past would be forgiven them,—it would impress me with desires that I might have a like blessed assurance.

My shop-mates finding that I had gained an introduction to other company, and that I had the advantage of spending my leisure time in respectable society, now began to see that the change which had taken place in me, was serious and settled; and they gradually became more respectful toward me. When I perceived this change in them, it opened the way again to mention to them their use of profane language. My remarks on that subject were now received very differently from what they had been before: and at length I had the satisfaction to see this evil habit wholly broken up. They, however, continued to wander about the streets of evenings, as before. In order to remove this habit, and to promote my own improvement, I adopted the practice of reading, writing, and attending to other branches of useful learning in the evenings. I perceived that this had an influence on them, and they became gradually drawn off from former habits into more regularity.

Our situation in the family was not so agreeable as among ourselves. We continued all days in the week to be accommodated in the kitchen; and as our dinner always came after the other parts of the family had dined, it was generally late. On first days it frequently interfered with, or came close on the time of our afternoon meetings. My care to be at meeting now began to be noticed by my master, and he would sometimes invite me to take dinner with him, that I might be at meeting in time. To this I always objected, unless my shop-mates came with me,—and gave him as a reason, that if we all dined together it would keep up the harmony among us.

At length I had the satisfaction to see the family all dine together on first days. No person who had never seen the consequences of a different practice, could conceive the advantages which followed this change. The happiness and convenience of the whole family were promoted by it; and the respect was increased between the master and his apprentices. There was a greater pleasure in attending to all his orders; and I could plainly discover that he enjoyed the time he spent in the shop, much more than formerly.

This agreeable change in my situation frequently excited my gratitude, and led to a hope that the days of trouble had come to an end;—and that if I continued to "walk by the same rule and mind the same thing," I should now have some satisfaction. But although the scene was changed as to the outward, and a foundation laid for improvement, it was not long before I became convinced that the days of my spiritual warfare were not yet accomplished. A controversy with outward difficulties had no sooner been removed, than other occasions for watchful attention presented. My natural love of amusement being restrained by the power of the Divine principle, so far as to separate me from the common pastimes of youth,—now took a different direction. I became fond of cheerful conversation; and supposed to myself (provided the subjects were well chosen) that there could be no harm in occasionally enjoying company in this way. For a time I did not discover that this disposition was precisely the same that had been restrained from other amusements. My fears began to be excited by this discovery: but I had opened a door to weakness, and renewed the work of repentance. I now saw that I must not indulge my natural fondness for amusement even when that amusement was free from every moral objection:—because it was necessary, to the end that those natural dispositions should be made subject, that I should cease to act in the natural will, and know a perfect concurrence with the Divine will. In which case, all that I could be free to do, I must know I was at liberty to do. But my selection of subjects for cheerful conversation, being done in the *natural will*, had not as a ground and principle, the love of virtue, and was therefore condemnable by that pure Principle of Divine light which had begun in me the work of perfect redemption.

On further reflection upon the cause of uneasiness, produced by this indulgence in cheerfulness, I have believed that my mind was at that time but little acquainted with the deceitfulness of human nature, or the natural man;—and that, had I been permitted to run out into a love of much conversation, in this ignorant and weak state,—it is most probable that a fondness would have grown up in favor of external enjoyments which would have very much interrupted that inward watchful state in which the heart of man is laid open, and all the secret motives to action are fully comprehended. I therefore believe that at that day it was a merciful interference of Divine Providence purposely intended to guard me from loss and danger, and to open my ear to discipline.

In the course of my experience, I have observed others who have begun well, and made many sacrifices; but who for want of keeping under the discipline of the cross, have been drawn out from a steady abiding with the gift; and although they have retained a fair outside, yet they have never deepened in the knowledge of themselves, nor become clear in their acquaintance with that *pure light* by which a knowledge of their duty could be made manifest.

When a greater degree of reserve was submitted to, and more seasons of recollection and silent introversion experienced, my mind was furnished with fresh openings into the knowledge of human nature, and its tendency to submit to temptations both of an outward and a secret nature. I now discovered how I had been deceiving myself, and how others were deceived. I had also in those quiet moments of reflection and silent waiting upon God, many new conceptions of the meaning and harmony of particular passages of the scriptures; and some appeared full of instruction that before seemed to contain but little that I could understand.

I likewise saw more clearly into the importance of that pure and spiritual worship, for which the soul of man is qualified, when inward quietude is gained; and which proves more fully to those who experience it, the immortality of man, than all the arguments which can be advanced by the ablest talents.

It was while my mind was held in this state of reserve, a clear impression was made upon it, that my duty in life was not to be confined to a private sphere; but that if I stood passive and faithful to the light of Truth, I should at some period be called to the work of the ministry. In my then infant state, I was willing to suppose this prospect embraced a service that was at a considerable distance. But ever after it opened before me, my mind was clothed with much awfulness, particularly in our religious meetings. I believed it was of great importance to myself and to the cause of righteousness, that I should make no mistake in relation to this serious subject. I felt a great care lest some deceptive principle might obtain an advantage over me, and that under its influence I might engage in a service that did not belong to the gifts I had received. I esteem it among the blessings of kind Providence to have had those cautionary considerations; and particularly so, that the prospect of this path of duty was opened a considerable time before I found any clear call to enter upon it.

At length, when the impression came, it was felt with much clearness. The subject was short, and in the eye of human wisdom, very simple. It was, to communicate to the assembly, That all the first-born throughout the land of Egypt died, before the king of Egypt would let the promised seed go out of bondage. But while I was trembling under the impression and deliberating upon the subject of rising to express it, the meeting closed. As the omission was not in consequence of any opposition to the call,—I felt no condemnation, and my mind was calm and easy. The next instance of a like impression was submitted to; and the serene and quiet state that I experienced after I sat down, amounted to full and conclusive evidence that I had not mistaken my duty.

In the exercise of the gift, I felt many fears arising from a consideration of the solemnity of the work; but as I kept humbly attentive to the Divine impressions, I found his grace was all-sufficient. There are, no doubt, diversities of gifts, as well as differences of administrations, and operations; but in my case, I always found that the communications which I was called to make, although they were preceded by a solemnity of feeling without distinct images or ideas of things,—yet when the moment for utterance arrived, the subject or burden of the Word, was clearly presented to my natural understanding: and the more calm and deliberate I was, the clearer the way opened before me. I could see with greater certainty the direction of the Light in its divisions and variations of the course of the subject before me,—and was also better qualified to determine when and where to close.

But when at any time, or from whatever cause, that deliberation and correctness of the understanding, were interrupted,—whether from fear of man, or from too much zeal,—the gift would be in the same proportion obscured, and the exercise in testimony, neither relieving nor satisfactory.

In all the experience I have had in the ministry, I have been convinced that much depends upon wholly relying on the all-sufficiency of Him who promised to be to his servants, both mouth and wisdom, tongue and utterance. But as, in every instance of the blessings of heaven, our wise Creator has left something for us to do, in order to come at the full enjoyment of them,—so I believe it to be in regard to the ministry of the gospel. The gift may be bestowed; but by the indolence or inattention of the servant, the materials for it to act upon may be wanting,—the means of improvement may be unoccupied: and, like the seed in a neglected soil, it may not be permitted either to flourish, or become distinctly known to others, in consequence of the obstructions to its growth, or the mixture of other things.

I have often thought that those who are called to the ministry in the Society of Friends, would be much more clear and satisfactory in their testimonies, if they were more attentive to the subjects which are opened to the mind in their silent moments. In that case the same Divine Light which brought them into view, would open a clear understanding of them: and subjects thus opened and explained to the mind, when delivered in testimony, would be clear and satisfactory; and being clothed with the energies and authority of the Spirit, they would be communicated to the assembly with that weight and baptizing influence which ever attends true gospel ministry.

Another consideration had much place in my mind, in relation to the important office of the ministry,—and that was the *manner*. I had observed among ministers in our Society, generally, a change from a natural tone of the voice to a manner of speaking that seemed unnatural. In this however there was much variety. Some spoke very loud and rapid. Others, though less rapid, used greater or less degrees of tone. Those tones or tunes were generally soft, and in some measure calculated to affect the passions,—especially when connected with mournful subjects. These variations from the natural tone of the voice became settled habits. From the powerful ascendency of these habits over many in their ministry, and from a consideration of the injury to their services in consequence of these habits, I was afraid of falling into any particular habit or manner of delivery. But with all the care I have taken to avoid the habits of others, my own manner has never been fully satisfactory; because I have not adhered to the natural tone of the voice, nor obtained the degree of deliberation that I could approve.

In the Society of Friends, there are persons in the station of Elders, who are particularly charged with the care of the ministry; and whose duty it is to point out where improvement is needed in the exercise of the gift. But is there not too much backwardness among Elders in mentioning to ministers what occurs for their improvement in this respect? Hence habits become formed for want of care in the Elders, and tones and gestures are used that hurt the service of ministers.

After my first appearing in the ministry, I remained an apprentice in the city about four years. In the course of this time, my situation outwardly was so similar that I have few remarks to make. But it is due to my numerous friends there to say, that they watched over me for good, and from them I received many excellent cautions, and much good counsel. It was to me a season of improvement; and I derived much benefit from the society I was favored to enjoy. In the situation in which I was placed with the family where I lived, I was furnished with many opportunities of viewing human nature, from which I also derived lessons of instruction: and from scenes which I witnessed there, impressions were made concerning the state of man when unsubjected to the Divine will, which I believe will be useful to me while I remain in mutability.

CHAPTER III.

His removal to East Caln—Settlement at Yorktown—Return to Caln, journey to Catawissa and Muncy—also to Carolina, &c.—Trials, in relation to special providence—Journey to New Jersey—Removal to Downingtown—Reflections—Concern to go to Europe.

About the close of the summer of 1789, the period arrived when I was at liberty to leave the city. Apprehending it would not be best to think of going into business there, I concluded to spend the fall and winter in Chester county. Accordingly, I parted with my friends and the family with whom I had lived in the city, and went into the neighborhood of East Caln, where I commenced keeping school.

The satisfaction which I felt on being at liberty from the service of another, and to engage in plans of my own, was a considerable gratification to me. But I soon found that difficulties were to be met with; and that now I was to engage for myself without means and without experience in the business of the world,—I had a very different state of concerns to manage from those of my apprenticeship. In my former situation, I had no contracts to make, no debts to pay, and no accounts to settle. The prospect of dangers from the exposure to the world, now made a deep impression upon me. I had noticed some who began well, and bid fair to be useful when they commenced business for themselves; but who soon lost their reputation by making engagements which they failed to comply with, and by running out into degrees of extravagance, which their means were not sufficient to support. Others again, who became so much taken up with their worldly concerns that they neglected their religious duties, and became cool in their love to the Divine Principle;—particularly when they were prosperous in business.

There is in the principle and the order of the Society of Friends, a limitation of expenses that seems naturally to open the way for worldly prosperity among the industrious. Some of the members who from proper motives have put on plain apparel, and who have begun poor in the world, being conscientiously concerned to keep within the bounds of their circumstances,—have, nevertheless, by a steady regard to correct principles and industrious habits, become prosperous: but at length, by giving way to a close disposition, in proportion to the increase of their temporal property, have acquired so much love of the world, and attachment to their interest, that they have become cool in their love of the Truth. And though some of these retain a fair and plain outside, and are punctual to their promises and exact in the payment of their debts,—yet through covetousness, they have lost the dew of their youth, and been but barren members of society. When we look into the families of some of these, we find among them and their children, that their conversation is very much confined to the world, and they feel but little interest in religious subjects. They are, in their own estimation, so moral and whole that it is exceedingly difficult to reach them, or convince them that they are lacking the inheritance of the pure life of Truth.

Under some of these views, and the dangers attending worldly pursuits, I had many fears lest, after all I had known of the mercy and goodness of a gracious Father and Almighty Friend, I might fall into weakness and entanglements. But from the pressure of difficulties which I experienced for several years, my mind was kept humble and dependent. And I now believe, it was much safer, and tended more to my preservation, to be poor in my beginning in the world, than if I had commenced in the midst of plenty, and with larger prospects before me.

In the course of the winter, I made up my mind to settle in Yorktown in the spring. Having contracted an acquaintance with Elizabeth, the eldest daughter of Moses Coates, we were united in marriage in the early part of the year 1790. It was a connection entered into with the consent of all parties concerned, and has proved to be a great blessing to me.

After removing to my native place, I began the requisite preparations for carrying on my trade. But with all the exertions I could make, the principal part of the summer was past, before I could get in readiness. And having to borrow money on interest, to begin with, I felt this disappointment to be a great disadvantage to me in my first attempts to go into business. The propriety and necessity of fulfilling all the contracts I made, was what I fully admitted; but the delay experienced in getting into business, and the unavoidable expenses to which I was subject, landed me in great discouragement; so that I began to fear that my creditors would suffer by me. In the midst of my fears, and at a time when my concerns wore a doubtful appearance as to what might be their issue, a report was spread by a member of Society, that I was so much entangled in my circumstances, that I must fail. By this means, some who had given me credit, were induced to demand the payment of their money. I knew not the cause at the time. But having always made payments when they were demanded, I resorted to my usual practice of borrowing, —under promise of returning the money again at a time mentioned to the lender. But to my surprise I found a kind of hesitation in persons who before had been free, and ready to oblige me. At length, the explanation came out, and there was no difficulty in learning who was the author of the report.

Under these trials, I was almost ready to despair of maintaining the standing which I believed was required by the principle of Truth, of which I had been making a public profession. My health also began to fail, from the close application that I paid to my business, and the pressure of concern under which I had been exercised. I saw too that the place I had chosen to commence business in, would not answer. In these circumstances, I called a number of my friends together, and opened to them my situation; at the same time letting them know, that I believed I could do better by returning to Chester county. After fully knowing how I was circumstanced, they advised me to try the place another year: and to this I submitted. But in the round of the year, I became fully convinced that a change was indispensable. I therefore had another opportunity with my friends, and let them know that if I remained among them, I must fail to fulfill my contracts, and thereby wound the profession I had been making. Some of them supposed that I was too easily discouraged; but others thought it would be best to leave me fully at liberty to look out for a different situation, if I should, on mature consideration, think proper to do so.

In the beginning of the year 1794, I went to the neighborhood of East Caln, in search of a place for myself and family. The kindness of my friends in assisting me to obtain the requisite accommodation, I still remember with gratitude. A tract of land and dwelling house were purchased at a moderate price, and I removed to East Caln in the spring of 1794.

Before I conclude the account of my residence at Yorktown, I may remark, that it seemed in many respects a critical and dangerous time to me. On the side of the world I had my trials. In the Society, my way seemed shut up. I could find few or none of the kind of company that I wished for. But, under all circumstances, my confidence was maintained in the care of Divine Providence over me. I believed in the promise, that they who "seek first the kingdom of God and his righteousness," shall have "all things" necessary added unto them. And at times in our religious meetings, I felt sensible that I was not forsaken. My mind was tendered under the assurances of Divine love to man; and in these seasons I could discover that it was all in wisdom that I was tried.

When I had returned to East Caln, I had to erect the necessary buildings for a shop and fixtures in which to carry on my trade of a potter: and had my health been equal to the business, it appeared for a time to be likely to answer for a livelihood. But in a few months I found my health was failing, and that I must decline the business, otherwise I should be hastened out of the world by it. Upon serious reflection,

I came to the conclusion to sell out the whole concern; which was accordingly effected without loss.

After having sold the property and being out of business, my situation was trying, and I sometimes felt much discouraged. I next rented a tenement and lot on which there was a building that answered for a school house, and in which I concluded to open a school. I commenced accordingly; but very soon after, I was impressed with a belief that it would be right for me to leave home, in order to make a religious visit to Friends of Roaring Creek, Catawissa, Fishing Creek, and Muncy. This being the first instance of my concern to travel on Truth's account, and having made a beginning in teaching the school, it was a close trial to leave my family and business at a time when I had as it were, just made a new beginning in the world, and when I knew the means I had were very small. But feeling the impression to be weighty, I resigned myself to the duty; and having the unity of Friends in the order of society, I set out on the journey, having William Mode as my companion.

In the course of this visit, my confidence in the safety of submitting to the clear openings of duty, was in no degree lessened. On attending one of the monthly meetings, I heard the report of a committee concerning two Friends, who were said to be at open variance, and that they saw no hope of their being reconciled. I afterward learned that both these Friends had large families; and it was evident to me that if they continued at variance, it would not only destroy their own comfort, but be of great disadvantage to their families. As I felt much exercised on the occasion, at length it opened to me as a duty, to see the two families together at their meeting house. They accordingly came together; and after sitting silently with them for some time, my way opened to remark to the young people, that I was sorry to hear that their parents were not on friendly terms with each other;—and that I hoped (however their parents might unwisely remain at variance,) they would by no means suffer themselves to entertain such feelings in their hearts, but cherish a disposition of kindness and good will toward one another;—and this might render them instruments for restoring unity and friendly feelings between their parents. But, should the parents continue to cherish hard thoughts, and unkindness toward each other, and even blindly go down to the graves in this state (which I sincerely hoped would not be the case,) I earnestly advised and admonished the children to take warning by the awful circumstance.

Having thus opened my concern to them, as Truth led the way, I had cause to rejoice in that it took such hold of the Friends at variance, that they became friendly to each other, and mutually concluded to drop all former causes of uneasiness, and in Future to live as Friends should do.

This was one of the cases that served to convince me, that it is not in man (by his own powers alone) to lead his brother out of a fault,—and that this can only be done by the truly spiritual-minded man, under the qualifying influence of the wisdom that cometh from above.

This visit was performed in four weeks: and on my return to my family, I felt a quietude of mind which amounted to an ample reward.

While permitted to be at home, I knew it was my duty carefully to attend to my temporal concerns. This I endeavored to do with all the diligence of which I was capable: but my constitution being delicate, and in some measure injured by the business I followed, it became necessary to decline it. Hence I was induced to sell the property I had purchased, and as it were, begin the world anew. But there was some difficulty in deciding upon what business to follow. After many thoughts on the subject, I concluded to employ the time at keeping school, until something more adapted to my choice should offer. While engaged in this occupation, I felt my mind drawn to a concern of paying a religious visit to some parts of Maryland, Virginia, and North Carolina. The prospect was serious in every view that I could take of it. I had now two children to provide for, and still remained poor.

But the concern rested with so much weight on my mind, that I was most easy to spread it before my Friends. They appointed a committee to confer with me upon it; and to this committee I opened my situation. After fully deliberating on the prospect, it was united with. In conformity therewith I made the best arrangement I could for the journey. My temporal concerns were now brought to a very limited state; and (except the articles of household furniture) what I had was in money,—the amount of which I divided, taking one half to bear the expenses of the journey, and leaving the other half to accommodate my wife and children in my absence.

In the fulfillment of this religious duty, I was from home three months, and travelled seventeen hundred miles. The journey was performed in the fall of the year 1795; and in the course of it, I attended the Yearly Meeting of Friends in North Carolina. It gave me an opportunity for much reflection, and was a time of instruction. I saw that some seemed to overact their part, and by taking hold of too much, they lost the weight and influence, which they otherwise might have had. I saw too that where any meddled beyond their depth, such were not even credited with what they seemed to know. Upon the whole the Meeting was well conducted, and furnished occasion to believe that there were many valuable members belonging to it.

Of this journey I kept some account. After attending the Yearly Meeting, my stay was short in that part of the country. On my way home I had several meetings, and visited a man in prison who was under sentence of death for horse stealing. When I arrived at home, it was my happiness to find my dear wife and children in good health.

On my return home, the school was ready to engage my attention: but finding that the compensation was not sufficient for the support of my family, I was not satisfied to remain in it. On this occasion some of my friends were uneasy with me; charging me with a want of steadiness; and alleging that while I was unwilling to continue in a business for which (in their opinion) I was qualified, I could not expect they would be disposed to do any thing for me. In return, I remarked that the compensation was not sufficient; but if they would make it so, I would not quit the business. I let them know that unless they would pay me what I believed was right, I should look for other business. Accordingly, I declined teaching the school; and although I saw no way to get along, and was sensible of the prejudice which would attach to me for so doing, it yet seemed right for me to leave.

During the interval that passed after this event, and before I became engaged in business again, to my mind, I was subject to many discouragements. During this period also, a visit was paid to my family by a company of Friends who were out on that service. They were Friends that I respected. My situation at that time was unusually gloomy; and the communications of those Friends were singularly calculated to increase my discouragements. On parting with them I felt much sunk, and ready to conclude that some unhappy mistake had been made on my part;—and therefore I should find no further way to open for my comfort or success in the world.

Under these impressions, and the pressure of my temporal difficulties, my faith in the special providence of the Almighty became in some measure weakened. Hence arose a general consideration of the doctrine of Divine revelation to man. I saw that with this doctrine was connected a belief in his particular providence: that is, that every revelation which had been claimed, either by Jews or Christians, must be associated with a belief in such a providence. From those reflections and considerations, my ideas became so mixed and perplexed, that I began to doubt whether there was any degree of certainty to be obtained. If, said I, there is no special or particular providence, then there can be no revelation;—and if no revelation, there can be no certainty;—and if no certainty, there can be no accountability: and therefore the whole state of man must be generally misunderstood. To talk about *certainty*, as resulting from our natural powers only,—or to suppose they were capable of arriving at it, argues decided ignorance of our capacities. This was evident to me from a full conviction that the organs of intelligence to the natural man, were the five senses. I knew that each of these might be deceived: and therefore, that they could not be the instruments of correct intelligence to the understanding. I considered, too, that unless revelation was believed in, all the ideas that were excited by the operation of the natural senses, could never prove the doctrine, either of eternal existence, or the immortality of man.

But all these perplexities of thought happily subsided, and my mind became settled in a full and satisfactory belief, that *there could be no effect without a cause*;—and that *every effect must agree* with its own particular cause. All ideas, therefore, that were excited, must agree with their exciting causes;—those that were natural, with natural causes;—and those that were spiritual, with spiritual causes. The idea, therefore, that "God is a Spirit,"—must have had a supernatural origin; and consequently that at some period there must have been a revelation of this idea. My faith in communications of a spiritual and supernatural kind, was now renewed; and I could find in myself particular impressions and feelings, which I was satisfied were not the result of natural causes. By these, I was much more powerfully convinced of the truth of revelation, than by any reasoning upon the subject.

Having been favored to rise above those doubts and

fears, which had almost destroyed my confidence in the particular providence of the Almighty,—my heart became enlarged, as at other times, in love to all mankind, and melted into tenderness under a sense of the love of God. New prospects of journeys and engagements for the promotion of righteousness, were also opened before me.

My next journey after that to Carolina, was through parts of New Jersey. It was a little singular, that in many of the meetings I was at in this journey, I felt engaged to hold up such evidence as had served to satisfy me, of the truth of Divine revelation. But by the information that I afterward received, I was made easy on this subject. It appeared that many had been led into doubts, by the reading of a libertine work which had been published not long before.

On my return from this journey, my mind was much comforted in a persuasion that the time had been rightly devoted. This little tour was accomplished in about six weeks. After my return home, I felt less pressure upon my mind from worldly considerations, than had been usual with me for some time before. I believed that if I kept in the patience, and did what I found to do, both in temporal and spiritual concerns, there would be a way made for me. Under these ideas, it was possible to feel contented, without seeing far before me; and I was often instructed by reflections on the necessity and value of true faith.

From this time circumstances began to change, and prospects gradually to brighten before me. In the spring of the year 1797, I was accommodated with a farm in the neighborhood of Downingtown, upon terms which were peculiarly generous: and which I believed I might, with care and industry, in time be able to pay for. To it I removed and settled; and soon after became a member of Uwchlan monthly meeting. My attention was now drawn to the business of the world; and I thought I felt a degree of necessity to exert myself in order to make the new plan of business answer a good purpose. By perseverance in the management of the farm, I was soon convinced that it was possible for the mind to become so very much engrossed, as even to loose sight of more important objects of thought. But notwithstanding this, it must be granted, that to a mind kept under the government of correct principles, there is perhaps no occupation which is better calculated to lead into a dependence on Divine Providence: for the husbandman practically learns, that though "Paul may plant and Apollos water, yet it is God who gives the increase."

Between the years, 1797 and 1804, I performed religious visits to several different places; and the gradual improvement of my farm opened the agreeable prospect, that the time would arrive when my situation in the world would be more favorable.

Upon a retrospect of the past, I have admired the wisdom of Divine Providence in suffering me to feel so much pressure, and occasions for so many fears and trials, in relation to my temporal concerns. Had my case been a more independent one, I now have no doubt that the notice and attention which I received among the respectable members of society would have raised in me a spirit of self-importance, which is opposed to the humility necessary for a Christian, and dangerous to a minister of the gospel.

Hence, I have concluded that our condition in the world is not a mere case of accident: but that the blessed Author of our being comprehends the make of each mind, and appoints to every one the kind of station that is suited to his probationary state. I also see that it is possible for the hand of benevolence to be extended in cases where it would be better for the individual to be very much left in the station or condition providentially allotted him. The very circumstances of those who have to apply themselves with diligence to business, are no doubt often the means of furnishing, in addition to the situation of humble dependence, a fund of practical knowledge, and a field of necessary discipline. So far as my observations have been made upon the most interesting and useful members of civil and religious society, I find them generally to be persons who have had but small beginnings in the world. And it has been evident to me, that their minds have become strong, vigorous, and well-informed, by means of the steady application which their circumstances have called for. It is possible that young persons, under right discipline and a correct form of education, may be so enlightened as to be preserved from indolence, even though placed in the inheritance of ease and opulence. But where necessity for application is taken away, it requires more than a common mind to conquer the temptations to indulgences which are inimical to the acquirement of useful and experimental knowledge.

Under these considerations, a solicitude to place my children in circumstances of independence, has been very much removed; and I have preferred giving them a plain, practical education. Young people who are brought up in business, and who become attached to it, are much more likely to be kept from bad habits, than those who are indulged in idleness. And I esteem the condition of a young man who has but little wealth, and who is well acquainted with business,—much more promising than that of those who are left in the possession of wealth, and in habits of idleness.

As the terms on which I had purchased my farm, were particularly favorable, and the time for closing the contract so distant as to furnish a hope that I might succeed in making it my own,—I felt solicitous to devote my time to that object: and therefore was willing to suppose that no religious duty could occur which would interfere with my plans. But to my disappointment and trial, which seemed very great to me, a prospect presented that it was my duty to stand resigned to go on a religious visit to some parts of England, and to Ireland generally. When this prospect fastened seriously upon me, I took into consideration the probable consequences in relation to the purchase I had made, and I could see no other way (if I went the journey) than that it must defeat all hopes of success in my temporal prospects. The trial was great, not only as it related to my temporal affairs, but also in regard to parting with my wife and children; and it seemed impossible to bring my mind to a state of resignation.

But at length, finding that my peace of mind was involved in the concern, and that nothing short of giving up to the prospect would leave it at rest, I communicated the subject to our monthly meeting. The concern was united with, and a certificate was granted on the occasion. The prospect was next opened to the Quarterly meeting, and on solid deliberation, it was also there united with, and the unity of the Quarter certified by an endorsement upon the certificate of the monthly meeting. It was then laid before the Yearly Meeting of ministers and elders, where it was not fully united with, and I was released from the concern, and permitted to remain at home.

The comfort I felt on this occasion is not very readily described. I now began to have my hopes revived that I should be permitted to pursue my temporal business until I had laid a fair foundation for a comfortable living for my family. But although in the order of society I had been excused from going on the extensive journey that had opened to my view,—yet it was not long before the concern returned, and I was constrained to lay it before Friends again. It was now united with, and I was set at liberty to pursue the prospect before me, as Truth might open the way.

Accordingly, in the 7th month, 1804, I parted with my family and worldly pursuits, with the entire unity of the society, and set out on my journey to Europe.

CHAPTER IV.

Voyage to Liverpool—Travels in England and Ireland—Return home—Reflections—Visit to Philadelphia—Reflections—Journey to the South, to visit Slaveholders—Visit to Philadelphia.

In my voyage to England, I sailed in the ship Annowon, Captain Thomson. There were several cabin passengers beside myself: one of the men was an officer of the British government, and I found him to be a person well informed, and an agreeable companion on the voyage. We were twenty-five days in crossing the Atlantic, and the weather was favorable all the time, except about eight hours, when the wind blew strong, and I had an opportunity of witnessing its force at sea. While on the passage, I felt best satisfied to inform the captain, that I believed it would be right for me to propose having a meeting with the ship's company. He fully approved the proposal, and it was gladly embraced by all the company. It was accordingly held, and was a favored opportunity.

After landing at Liverpool, I went to the house of Isaac Hadwin. He and his wife Susanna, were both useful and valuable Friends. While here, I had the satisfaction of being called upon by a number of Friends, whose society I found very interesting. Among the number, a widow Benson and two of her daughters came, and spent part of an afternoon. She said she had another daughter who uniformly shunned the company of Friends in the ministry. I concluded there must have been a cause for this singular conduct, and I would see if I could not get to understand it.

Accordingly, the first time I went to the house, I found her in the parlor, and spoke to her in an open and sociable manner. To prevent her from making an escape, I remarked that they had a pleasant garden, and I should like to look into it, and see whether I could find any of my American acquaintance there. The younger daughters were at once ready to go with me, but Rachel seemed to lag behind. I objected to going, unless we all went. She then consented to go; and I embraced the opportunity to inform her, that I understood she had uniformly shunned the company of Friends in the ministry; and as this was a new kind of a case, I would be glad to understand the cause, if she was free to inform me: but I would not urge her to an explanation, if she was not willing.

She seemed a little embarrassed at first; but after a few minutes she concluded to inform me of her reasons. She said that from her childhood she had a fondness for dress; and although she had never been extravagant, nor more expensive than her sisters,—yet there was some gaiety in her general appearance; and this circumstance was sufficient to produce remarks upon her, which she did not feel prepared to meet: and therefore, in order to escape from having her feelings hurt by such attacks upon her, she had for some time past chosen to keep out of the way.

In my reflections upon this case, I have been instructed; being convinced that it is necessary to be very careful how we meddle with those external subjects. Under the influence of impressions made by the sight of the eye, we may be induced to make remarks without any proper qualification: and thus excite prejudices which may remain for a length of time, and only tend to drive the young and inexperienced mind further off. So far as my experience has gone, I have found that every thing done under the di-direction of the Divine guide, has a tendency to gather into the blessed unity of the one spirit, and bond of peace.

After remaining at Liverpool about two weeks, way opened in my mind to visit the meetings of Friends at the following places, namely, Warrington, Manchester, Stockport, Morley, Macclesfield, Leek, Mansfield, Derby, Nottingham, Leicester, Sheffield, Ackworth, and York. At the last mentioned place, I met with Lindley Murray, who appeared to be a man of a large and liberal mind.

From York I returned to Liverpool; and after resting a few days, I went to Holy Head, and thence crossed the Irish sea to Dublin. Here I was kindly accommodated at the house of Jonas Stott. I attended the meetings in Dublin; but my mind was much closed up, and there seemed no way to obtain any relief. After attending a number of their meetings in silence, my mind was at length opened in a view of the perfection of our form of meeting in silence. I remarked that it was incapable of reform: that is, that no form of meeting together for the purpose of Divine worship could be more perfect than that of meeting in silence; and therefore it was impossible to make any improvement upon this form. Thus also, I observed it was with the profession of Friends, there could be no improvement of the principle.

In the meeting where those views were opened, I felt a calm, and a precious reward of peace. But in the afternoon, when I was present at another meeting, an elderly Friend got up and mentioned that our

American Friend had stated in the morning meeting, that such was the perfection of our form of meeting in silence, that it admitted of no reform. But that he said nothing about the duty of meeting together, which he thought at the time was an omission, and it was now brought into notice for amendment. But I did not think myself bound at that time to speak to the case. When the meeting closed, I was spoken to by the elders on the subject. I told them that I never had attempted to minister in a meeting, at the direction of another; and that it would have been an error in me to have attempted it on the present occasion.

After spending about two weeks in Dublin, I proceeded towards the South of Ireland, visiting a number of small meetings, and finding very little that was encouraging. At Edenderry I met with Jane Watson who had been in America in the service of the ministry; but was at this time set aside from the station in which she had stood. From Edenderry I went on visiting the meetings as far as Cork. In most places, the society appeared to be on the decline. I then proceeded by the way of Youghal, Ross, and Roserea, to Clonmell. Here, I met with several valuable members, and Friends in this place seemed to have some weight and influence. At Clonmell I found Mary Dudley, Sarah Grubb (formerly Lynes) and her husband John Grubb, a widow Pern, and a number of others.

After spending near a week in Clonmell, and the neighborhood, I proceeded to Waterford, and went thence to Carlow. From Carlow I went to Ballitore; and found but little to encourage me, among the few

Friends that met with Abraham Shackleton, who went among the dissenters.

Abraham Shackleton insisted on my going to see his family. Soon after I sat down in his house, he handed me Milton's Paradise Lost, and opened it at a picture of a serpent with an apple in its mouth, tempting a woman;—and asked me what I thought of that. I answered that I did not consider myself a judge of the picture: I could not say whether it was well executed, or not. He remarked, that was not the object he had in view by handing me the book. What did I think of a serpent's tempting a woman with an apple? I told him the idea appeared to me to be an awkward one. I did not think there was a woman in a thousand, that would feel any temptation to take an apple out of the mouth of a snake. Abraham then said, his object was to know my opinion as to the existence of an evil principle that envied the human race, and was constantly endeavoring to draw us out of the way in which we should go. To this inquiry I remarked, that I supposed he was so much of a philosopher as to admit that there was no effect without a cause. Of course, as there was evil in the world, it appeared to me not very material whether we understood whence it arose, or not;—or whether it proceeded from one or from many causes: our great business was, to get the better of it; and if we succeeded, it was all that need concern us on the subject. So he admitted the conclusion and dropped the matter.

After spending a short time at Ballitore, I returned to Dublin, and attended the Yearly Meeting there. Soon after this I found my mind turned back again to Liverpool. Accordingly, I parted with Friends there, and went on board a packet for Holy Head. Our passage was a very trying one, with the wind ahead nearly all the way; and we were about forty-eight hours in crossing, when in common it takes but ten or twelve.

When I arrived at Liverpool, I found new occasions of exercise. Friends had become divided into parties, and thus involved themselves in difficulties. The opportunities I had with Friends at Liverpool, went to convince me that I had been rightly directed in returning thither. But the cases I had to meet were trying; more especially as I had to act very much on my own judgment and feelings. In concluding the service there, it was cause of gratitude to part with Friends under the precious evidence of mutual love and regard.

After this, there seemed an opening to make a visit to London, that great city of pride and self-importance. I attended the Yearly Meeting of Friends held there; and it was deeply affecting to my mind, as I sat in those meetings, to observe men rising up and taking an active part in the concerns of Society, who appeared to act and speak exclusively from the mere powers of their own natural capacities. Hence, when a subject was under consideration, their method of coming to a conclusion seemed to me to be principally by argument. I inquired of the Meeting, whether, in the judgment of Friends, it was most in agreement with our religious profession, to decide upon cases that came before them, by argument,—or by simply attending to the sense of Truth in the minds of Friends, and accepting the generally prevailing sense for the conclusion. The Meeting took up the subject; and after considerable discussion came to the conclusion, that it would be better in all cases to be guided by the general sense of the Meeting.

After attending the Yearly Meeting, my way opened to have an appointed meeting in each of Friends' meeting houses in London; which was accordingly done, beginning at the Peel meeting, and ending at Radcliff. These opportunities were solemn and precious meetings; and at the close, I was thankful to feel my mind discharged from further service in this great city.

In my reflections while in London, I could not but believe, that if the pure principle of Divine wisdom had been followed, it would never have crowded so many human beings together, as are in that place. Those who have been brought up in the country, and are acquainted with the business of a country life, would do well seriously and deliberately to consider their motives for going into cities, before they determine to remove there.

Seeing my way open to proceed to Bristol, I went and had an interesting meeting there. After which it appeared right for me again to go to Ireland. I accordingly went, and visited the meetings of Friends generally in the north, and thence proceeded southward to Dublin. It was sorrowful to find that Friends were few in number in that nation; and there was but a gloomy prospect in relation to the advancement of our Christian testimonies in those parts.

While I was in the north, I met with several who had been active members in the Society, that were now turned away from Friends, and were evidently dwindling into mere blanks. Of this I was fully convinced by the various visionary opinions and notions which some of them professed to entertain.

It was also affecting to meet with so many poor, distressed fellow creatures as abounded in that country. I found, when I mentioned the condition of the poor, that those who were faring sumptuously every day, could remark very coolly, that if the poor had salt and potatoes, they would do very well.

My stay in Ireland was not long. Soon after I reached Dublin, I felt at liberty to part with Friends of that country, and took my passage for Holy Head. There were about forty passengers on board, and we had an awful time in crossing the Irish channel. As we seemed likely, by contrary winds, to be driven among the rocks on the British shore, there was great alarm among the passengers: and a number of them began to make confession of their many sins. The captain, however, with much difficulty turned his vessel to sea; and, though it was very rough, yet we seemed out of danger of being thrown on the rocks. Next morning we came safe to shore.

Finding that my prospects in England were not likely to be enlarged. I believed the time for embarking for my native land was nearly arrived; and it was a great satisfaction to be permitted to look towards returning to my family.

In passing through the different towns in England, my mind was frequently brought under great discouragement, in relation to the promotion of the cause of Truth, and the advancement of our christian testimonies,—so many and various are the customs that stand in the way. I saw that there were many large manufactories which are owned by the wealthy; while the poor are altogether dependent, and are closely confined to labor, and that for a very small compensation. In common, they are paid their week's wages on seventh day evening. After getting their money, they have to go to market; and many of them are out at market until a late hour.

In the beginning of the 7th month, 1805, I took passage in the ship Hercules, Captain Bradford. We crossed the ocean in forty-two days; and our passage was attended with but few unpleasant circumstances. The captain was a practical seaman, and prudent in the command and management of all that required his attention. I found my dear wife and family all well, which, with their and my preservation, inspired me with gratitude to the author of all our sure mercies.

The circumstances of this journey were such as gave me a liberal opportunity of understanding the state of the Society of Friends in England and Ireland. It was clear to me, that Friends in both nations had lost ground in many respects. I could see that their meetings, particularly those that were held on working, or business days, were small,—more especially on the men's side of the house. This was doubtless the consequence of a worldly spirit gaining place with many of them. Among the excuses for this neglect, some of them would remark that they would love to attend their meetings, but their temporal situation was such that it required a very careful attention, in order to get along with satisfaction;—alleging that they had many expenses to support and that these must be met and rightly managed, or their condition would become uncomfortable to themselves and their families.

But the difficulty seemed to me to be more the effect

of expensive habits of living, than from any other cause. Another source of weakness, and what appeared likely more and more to rob Friends of their strength, was their becoming fond of the flattery of the world. I perceived they were taking part in Bible societies, and other apparently plausible institutions that were sanctioned by the clergy in that country. Thus Friends seemed to think that by letting go some of the peculiarities of the society, they and other professors might come together more than had formerly been the case. But Friends in England appeared to forget that they had been called upon from their first rise to stand separate from all others—and one ground of this may be seen in the fact that Friends do stand alone in the acknowledgment of a Divine gift of Light and Truth, given to every man to profit withal; that is, they believe in the immediate revelation of the Divine will to man.

On the 18th of the 2d month, 1808, I left home with a prospect of having meetings in Philadelphia; my concern being chiefly to those who were not professors with us. In my ride to the city I was in some degree incommoded by the falling of abundance of rain. My mind was not much unlike the day,—attended with alternate storms and clouds. The idea of having to appoint a number of meetings in the city among people of very different descriptions, I have no doubt gave rise to this tumultuous and unpleasant state. In the evening a greater share of calmness was attained, and the sweetening spring of resignation, was like the clear sunshine of a summer evening, when the horizon is fair and serene.

19th.—With the opening of the morning, a little

spiritual light seemed to break forth, in which I saw the city and its inhabitants in districts; and the first step necessary to be taken in the concern before me. I proceeded accordingly, and called a few Friends together at the house of our valued elder, James Pemberton. To them was opened the engagement I felt, and the difficulties that appeared in my way. Like brethren, they entered into the concern, and were willing to aid in its prosecution. I proposed, that my first meeting be at Pine Street meeting house; and, if way should open, to renew the appointments at that house until the inhabitants at the south end of the city should all have had opportunity to be present. The prospect was united with, and provision was made to carry it into effect. We then parted, and I retired to my quarters and to my prayers, endeavoring to resign myself and the cause to my Divine Helper.

20th.—When I awoke this morning, my thoughts were turned to the days when the gospel was vocally preached by Jesus Christ to a dark and superstitious world. I opened the book and read the sacred record of his blessed doctrines;—and I said to myself, surely, with all the multitude of sentiments which have been marked upon the thousands of volumes that have been written,—a man may be wearied;—but with the superior and sacred doctrines which this volume contains, none need be weary, or fail to be edified! I was particularly interested in reading the incomparable sermon delivered upon the mountain, and most of all my attention was drawn to that part, "Consider the lilies: they toil not, neither do they spin: and yet I say unto you that even Solomon in all his glory, was not arrayed like one of these."

My attention was next arrested by reading a passage in Buffon's Natural History. The subject was the fluidity of matter, and its change under the different degrees of heat and cold. Soon, however, my thoughts passed the boundary of natural elements, and entered into a comparison of these with spiritual realities. By heat it appears that matter is rendered fluid, and is consequently less subject to the laws of attraction. By cold, it is made dense, and brought back again to the earth. So, by the warming influence of the *love of God*, the soul is expanded, and drawn out of the government of earthly attraction. By the chilling influence of the world's friendship, it is contracted and brought back to the earth.

I then went to meeting, and was engaged in speaking to a crowded assembly, on the subject of our Lord's address to the Jews: "If the Truth make you free, then are ye free indeed." It was a blessed opportunity, and was attended with the love of the gospel.

22d.—Now opens a new morning, and with it another day to be well or ill spent. The light upon the candlestick, and the division of light from darkness, —were the subjects that drew forth my mind in a stream of gospel affection among my friends at the North meeting: and the savor of the kingdom gave boldness to approach the throne of God in prayer, that his blessing might be upon the members of his militant church, and that they might, as the candlestick, hold up the Light they had received,—maintaining, with all meekness, the testimonies which connect with the gospel.

In the afternoon. The call of Jesus Christ to Simon whose surname was Peter, and Andrew his brother, who were casting their nets into the sea,—to come and follow him,—with the assurance that he would make them fishers of men,—was the subject spoken upon, in Market Street meeting house. It was a good meeting. In the evening meeting, I was silent.

23d.—In the meeting held this evening, I was favored with doctrine to deliver to a large assembly. It was a serious time,—and many minds were tendered. Next day had a precious opportunity at the North house, in which my concern for the dear children in our Society was feelingly expressed. I was led to call the attention of these to the necessity and duty of obedience to parents, and to the importance of keeping their tender consciences clear of guilt. I referred to the bad language frequently heard along the streets of Philadelphia, and mentioned my hope that they would not fall into that evil practice.

25th.—I was drawn into a similar concern for the children, at Pine Street meeting; which was opened, and appeared to have a happy effect. In the evening, I was present at a large public meeting in the North house. It was an interesting and solemn time.

Next day I attended the middle meeting; where my mind was again engaged in the cause of universal righteousness. A part of my concern in public testimony was for the children of Friends. Great tenderness accompanied my own mind, and it spread through the assembly.

In the evening, I was again engaged with a numerous auditory at the North house. The first part of my communication was doctrinal, and consisted principally in defending the belief, that the Divine Light was universal;—and that man was left free, having full power given him to obey, or disobey;—that sin was connected with disobedience, and could not otherwise have an existence;—that righteousness proceeded from the opposite course, and could only be manifested by our obedience to the revealed will of God. Having proved the absolute correspondence of this doctrine with the Holy Scriptures, and the clear consistency of it with an enlightened understanding,—way opened to take notice of some of the evil habits too common in this city; particularly such as were the means of separating men from their families, and leaving disconsolate women to lament their own, and the unhappy condition of their children. The interesting importance of my concern had a solemnizing effect, and a precious silence covered the meeting when I took my seat.

Next day, I attended the monthly meeting of Friends at the Middle district; and the day following had another public meeting in the new meeting house on Mulberry Street. A large number came together, and it was an opportunity in which, although I had much labor, there was but little relief.

3d mo. 1st.—Had a meeting in Southwark,—a precious opportunity, in which the gospel spring was opened, and many of the assembly, I believe, were glad they were there. I also attended the evening meeting in the new house, and was drawn forth in the flowings of tender concern among them. My testimony was plain, and I trust authorized by a measure of the baptizing power of Truth. A precious silence was spread over the meeting.

On the 3d, I was again at the North meeting, which was satisfactory In the evening I had a serious opportunity with the inhabitants of Kensington. Next morning I attended Pine Street meeting, and had a meeting there in the evening. In the last, I had much labor in the gospel, and it ended comfortably; leaving a hope that the exercise would not be lost among the people.

5th.—I again attended the meeting at Friends new meeting house on Mulberry Street; where I took a review of my religious engagements in the city, and it excited gratitude to my all-sufficient Helper. As the evening meeting approached, many discouragements arose in my mind, and I was nearly landed in a state of disqualification for the occasion. Under such impressions I went; and a numerous assembly was collected in the Market Street meeting house. It was not long after I had taken my seat, before every cloud vanished, and way opened to engage their attention on the necessity of yielding obedience to the Divine Word, or Light of Christ within. It was a serious time, and ended with much satisfaction.

Next day, I had a large meeting at the new house, where the way opened to treat of the true knowledge of God. The people were very attentive, and it ended with solemnity.

I now felt at liberty to return home; and accordingly set out and arrived there the next day.

4th mo. 4th.—I spent this day in attending to the improvement of my yard and garden. While thus employed, I was frequently occupied with thoughts on the importance of improving the mind; and it appeared to me that the more I am redeemed from all that pertains to the creature,—the better I shall understand the mind and will of the Creator concerning me. I was also persuaded that the soul is capable of attaining such an intimate knowledge of the Divinity, as to feel his presence and power; and in that power to withstand every appearance of evil When such a Divine union is gained, all things stand in the Light, as in the glare of eternal day;—the past, the present, and the future, are all equal and similar. In this state, time seems scarcely to have an existence. Nor is the faculty of reason so much the source of enjoyment, as that of spiritual sensation: though even reason (or the rational faculty) is rendered more clear, because the effusion of spiritual sensation commands a silence of all the passions, and thereby furnishes to this faculty a complete equanimity. In this exalted state, no bias prevails; but true and positive evidence is comprehended, and the conclusions founded thereon cannot fail to be correct.

6th.—Some attention has been paid to day to my books and accounts. It has served to convince me that the better plan would be to adopt the practice of settling my accounts, at least once in the year. I have observed, that in most of the disputes about property which have come within my knowledge, the accounts have been of long standing.

7th.—At our monthly meeting. In the forepart, my attention was drawn to the state of the meeting, and whilst I was musing, the fire burned. Hence arose an impression, under which I was engaged to speak; and the subjects presented with satisfactory clearness. During our attention to the business, I could not but marvel at what appeared to me to be the weakness of wise men, and the imperfections of society.

10th mo. 4th.—I left home with a prospect of attending Baltimore Yearly Meeting, and also of paying a visit to a few towns southward of that place. Lodged the first night at Jacob Lindley's, where the time was spent with satisfaction. Next day, went on till night overtook us, and we put up at a tavern kept by a widow Smith. While here, I could not but take notice of the effect of education. The widow regretted the bad habits of their neighborhood, and remarked that all the duties of the men seemed there to be neglected; and that hence they were deprived of many of the comforts of life common in Pennsylvania. And this difference was charged upon slavery.

On the 6th we arrived in Baltimore, and put up at Elisha Tyson's. On the 8th the Yearly Meeting of ministers and elders began. In the afternoon I was present at the meeting for sufferings; and was glad to find that the attention of Friends had been drawn to the situation of their members in the western country; and that they were awakened to the difficulties and hardships of opening and settling a wilderness country.

9th.—I attended in the morning the meeting at the west end of the city. It was large, and I felt engaged to call the attention of the people to our Christian testimony against wars and fightings. At the conclusion, I was satisfied; being persuaded that the assembly were ripe to receive and to reflect upon the important subject.

The business of the Yearly Meeting was transacted in harmony and to satisfaction. Among other things, the subject of the use of spirituous liquors received particular consideration.

On the 19th day of the 5th month, 1814, in conformity with a prospect which had for some time engaged my mind to pay a visit to the inhabitants of the Southern states, I this morning parted with my family.

It was more than a common trial to submit to this separation, as the weight of the engagement before me was particularly serious. In this journey I had Nathan Sharpless for a companion.

21st.—I was at the meeting of ministers and elders belonging to Warrington Quarterly Meeting. It was some consolation to me to find that I continued capable of feeling; but there was occasion to regret the defective state of the members of this meeting. On second day the 23d I attended the Quarterly Meeting, the business of which was conducted with a comfortable degree of unity. On the evening of the day, I had an interesting meeting with the black people; but it was injured by the unauthorized communication of a stranger.

The next evening I had a meeting with the people of York, which was a comfortable one, and tended to increase my attachment to them, and we parted in much good will.

26th.—I reached Baltimore, and attended the meeting at the east end of the city. Also had a meeting appointed for the inhabitants generally, which closed under a feeling of great solemnity.

28th.—On looking round and reflecting on my situation, I find but little relish for social conversation, and feel myself in a weak state. My faith in the all-sufficiency of the Principle is not in any degree shaken; but I have less confidence in myself than ever I knew before. It seems singular that I have no dependence on my own talents. On former occasions I have had a share of assurance that I might as a man meet men in general, without being under any apprehension of weakness appearing. But the case is now changed.

Infinite wisdom only comprehends the cause; but patience must have its perfect work.

29th.—This morning the meeting at the west end of Baltimore was in some degree comfortable. But much remains to be done before the Light of Truth will be preferred in all things, to the power of custom and the dominion of error.

Next day, rode to John C. Thomas's where an opportunity was had to observe the consequences of a change from holding slaves, to that of employing them as free men. By this change some attention to business by the family, was introduced; but years, no doubt, will roll away, before the habits consequent on slavery will be removed. Thence we went on to Washington.

On the 1st of the 6th month, I called on the President, and gave him some account of the prospect I had in view. He heard me attentively, and appeared to enter into the subject with some interest. He remarked that he had thought of the plan of removing the slaves to Africa as contemplated by Paul Cuffee; but many objections had occurred to him against it. He had also thought of their being colonized: but in this, difficulties also presented. In fact, difficulties would present in every plan that could be taken up. He said the only probable method that he could see, to remedy the evil,—would be for the different States of the Union to be willing to receive them; and thus they would be spread among the industrious and practical farmers, and their habits, education and condition would be improved. I felt a satisfaction to find that the subject had engaged his attention, and parted with him in an agreeable manner.

After attending Friends' meeting at Washington, I spent some time in the company of Doctor Thornton. He took considerable interest in our views, and presented me with a pamphlet on the subject of emancipation, which I read with satisfaction, because I found that this singularly persevering man had really felt the importance of the subject.

Next day we attended meeting at Alexandria to satisfaction. The necessity of faith in the Spirit of God, was the doctrine communicated. In the evening of the day following I had a meeting with the inhabitants generally.

In relation to the object of my concern, although difficulties seem to present on all hands, yet when I consider that every good work has had a beginning,—and that the blind were to be led in a way that they knew not, and in paths that they had not known,—I am led to hope that He who has all power in his hand, will provide a way, and work a deliverance for his afflicted creation, by means in his own all-powerful hands.

This evening I had some conversation with a young man who has travelled in several counties in Virginia. He stated, that so far as he could discover, there was a general preference to part with their slaves, provided it could be done to their advantage, and without too much loss on the part of those who hold them.

On first day, the 5th, I attended meetings at Alexandria, both fore and afternoon; both valuable opportunities. Next day, rode to Occoquan about fourteen miles, and put up with Nathaniel Ellicott. The weather came on wet and not fit for travelling,—a circumstance which taken in connection with the weight of impression that I felt, tended to furnish further evidence of the necessity of patience. How many are the occasions which present for the exercise of this virtue. But in no instance of my life, have I found it more requisite than at present.

On the 8th, I was at a meeting in the court-house at Dumfries. The assembly were remarkably silent, and attentive to the communication offered; and it was an opportunity in which I hope some profitable impressions were made. Next morning we left Dumfries and rode to Joseph Howard's, near Fredericksburg, and thence to Colonel Hugh Mercer's. After spending a little time with this man I felt most easy to inform him of my motives for travelling in Virginia. He heard me attentively, and appeared much interested. He particularly wished to know whether I had any plan in view for the general emancipation of the slaves. To this I answered,—that the subject was of great importance;—and that I wished more fully to comprehend all the difficulties that connected with it;—and that this I saw would require time. But that I could see so far as to be satisfied it was a subject of national concern, and would need the concentrated wisdom of the intelligent, to provide a safe and proper remedy. I hoped in the course of my journey to become possessed of a part of that wisdom by mingling with those who had reflected upon the subject.

The day following, I had a meeting with the inhabitants of Fredericksburg. It was not so large as I expected, nor did I find so much openness among the people, as in some other places. After parting with the assembly, it was some consolation to feel my mind calm and resigned. But I could not help thinking of the gloom that seemed to me to hang over this place; and which I believed was owing to the mass of iniquity among the people. Yet it is but just to say that they conducted steadily during the meeting, and I saw no external marks of disorder.

11th.—We left Fredericksburg, and rode to the neighborhood of Cedar Creek. On the way, we saw instances of black children without clothing; and passed over a country that appeared to be but thinly inhabited;—the soil poor, and the cultivation defective. The roads were much neglected, and the horses appeared much worn down. Next day, attended Cedar Creek meeting, and had a satisfactory opportunity. It was particularly so to find harmony among the members. We remained at Micajah Crew's until the 14th, when we went to Richmond, where I had an interview with George Hay. After opening my motives for wishing to see him, I discovered that he appeared under some embarrassment. But I informed him that I had no plan to propose,—that I particularly desired to learn whether, in the judgment of intelligent men of the South, the case was hopeless, and without remedy;—that if I found it so, I should conclude it was vain to devote further time to the subject. He preferred that I should obtain further and more general information; and I observed to him, that my motives for the present visit were not so much from a concern for the slaves, as for those who held them in possession;—that I felt for their situation, and the draw-back from comfort, to which they must be subject in consequence of their situation. He at length admitted that the slaves were a draw-back to their happiness, and we soon closed the conversation.

After this opportunity, I went to Friends' meeting, where I was comforted by a renewal of confidence in the simplicity and perfection of gospel ministry. Its perfections were contrasted with the mere mechanical movements of those who wait not for the Spirit. The meeting was solid and satisfactory.

In the afternoon, I had an interview with John Hopkins. He came out in an open, full confession, that to his certain knowledge, slavery was known and felt as an oppressive and grievous evil,—and that it was a circumstance which every sensible man in Virginia must and did regret. But they had been landed in it by their ancestors, and what way to obtain a safe and proper remedy, was the great question. Various views were taken relative to the mode of remedy: and it was evident that the further we pursued the subject, the more this man became impressed with desire that it might be pursued. He expressed a hope that I would extend my inquiries, and volunteered his offer to introduce me to a number of his acquaintances. After he had adverted to colonizing the slaves, as one expedient, and observed upon the difficulties which he supposed would follow an attempt of that kind,—he then stated a view that if the general government would take up the subject and provide funds to meet it, and let the slaves be spread over the United States—*that* had struck him as a plan which had the fewest exceptions, and no other method of remedy had presented to him with equal clearness.

My next interview was with G. K. Taylor, who was very free and open in conversation. He gave it as his opinion that if any plan could be devised that would promise a freedom from the cumber of slavery, he had no doubt (provided the same should be safe in its operation) it would be joyfully embraced. But that the subject was viewed as being hopeless; and therefore every expedient resorted to, was merely an effort to put the evil further off. He further remarked that if the northern citizens could be induced to view the concern as a national one, it might facilitate the perfection of a well-concerted plan. He could see no remedy short of the joint operation of the Union; and therefore believed that the National government would be the proper place for the subject to centre. The only remedy that he could expect would prove effectual, would go to spread the black population generally over the continent.

My next conference was with a judge who called upon me. He seemed much to wish that some way might open to remedy the evil; and remarked that those who were engaged on the subject should not be too anxious, but be willing to pursue it with patience and perseverance.

18th.—Our inquiries, so far as relates to Richmond, seem now to be brought to a close. Taking the result into view, it appears that one sentiment would be entertained upon the subject, if any plan were set on foot which promised a safe release from slavery;—and it is believed that such release can only be safely obtained by a union of efforts throughout the States; and therefore that it will be necessary for the subject to obtain the interference of the general government. The objections made to a partial emancipation, are founded upon the improper conduct of those that are set free. It is stated that they associate with the slaves, and through them have an opportunity to steal the property of slave holders: and hence they become idle and vicious. These statements present some views which may throw light upon the subject, and necessarily lead to a consideration of the causes of this general depravity.

19th.—In the forenoon, I was engaged among a numerous assembly of the inhabitants of Richmond, wherein it was cause of gratitude to believe that the Divine blessing was granted in solemnizing and profitably influencing the minds of many.

When I reflect upon the many discouraging thoughts that crowded upon me at the time of leaving home,—the fears that were entertained by my friends,—and the importance of the concern,—I feel an assurance that the Shepherd of Israel has mercifully opened the way in the minds of the people, to meet my concern; and a hope is entertained that, by patient perseverance, the foundation may be laid for a blessed termination to the evils of slavery.

20th.—I parted with Thomas Maule and wife, and proceeded on the way homeward to Micajah Crew's. It seems necessary to pursue every opening that may tend to promote the object of emancipation; confidently believing that way will be made safely to remove one of the greatest evils that ever the spirit of delusion has succeeded in imposing upon mankind.

22d.—Was present at Cedar Creek meeting. It was attended by a number who do not profess with us, and was a very interesting opportunity. Next day I attended Caroline meeting. Thence to Fredericksburg where I had an interview with Hugh Mercer. He appeared anxious to know the result of our visit to Richmond; and I could observe that it gave him satisfaction to be informed that we had been attended to with kindness, and that much interest was felt in the concern.

26th.—I attended a meeting appointed at Dumfries. It was large, and I was favored to spread before them the necessity of submission to the Divine Principle, in order to be happy. Much solemnity prevailed during the meeting, and at the conclusion there was a precious calm.

Thence we proceeded to Alexandria, where a meeting was had with the colored people; in which I was led, in much simplicity of doctrine, to address the assembly. They were very attentive, and sat in great quietude. I parted with them in much affection, and felt the same toward the citizens of Alexandria of respectable standing, who gave us their company on this interesting occasion.

The next day we went on our journey toward home, where we arrived on the 2d of the 7th month, 1814, and I found my family in a comfortable state.

After my return, I was at Westown boarding school, Darby and Philadelphia, and attended meetings as they came in course. I also attended the funeral of Mary Bonsal. The esteem in which she was held among her friends, was very manifest by the numerous and solemn procession that was present on the occasion.

7th. mo. 26th.—I was at the monthly meeting for the northern district, Philadelphia: The business of which, I thought, was conducted with more formality than was requisite. In the afternoon, I met a selected company of Friends, to whom I communicated the result of my late journey, as it related to the great subject of slavery. I did not think that they felt it in either its force or importance, so fully as will one day be necessary. Next day I spent some time with George Logan with considerable satisfaction. The subject of slavery was entered upon, and I was pleased to find that it had engaged his serious attention. He professed a willingness to aid me in any way that I thought he might be useful.

The two following days, I devoted some time to the examination of a manuscript which I had submitted to the Meeting for sufferings.

30th.—I was present with the Quarterly meeting of ministers and elders in Philadelphia. In this opportunity I felt much for the preservation of love and unity among Friends; and took notice, that in the same proportion this was maintained, they would be a blessing to each other, and brighten in the exercise of their several gifts.

Next day I was at Mulberry Street meeting, and felt some satisfaction in a silent attention to the state of my own mind,—the leadings of the principle,—and the solemnity of the meeting; but had little to communicate to the assembly.

8th. mo. 1st.—I was deeply impressed with considerations on the state of society, and the necessity there was for a more perfect separation from the love of the world.

Having remained on the farm near Downingtown about twenty years, I found it was not possible for me to make the property my own, as originally contemplated,—but that I was getting more and more in debt every year. I therefore thought it would be best to sell it while land was bringing a fair price. But on consulting my friends of the neighborhood, they were not willing I should leave the parts. I therefore omitted selling, and the price of land soon after commenced falling; so that when I was obliged to sell, I could obtain only about half the sum I had been offered for it seven years before. So great a fall in the price of property left me in debt, after parting with nearly all the substance I possessed. Had I sold the farm for the sum offered me, at the time I believed it right to sell, I should have been able to pay all my debts, and have a competency left for my support and that of my family.

From the time of my commencing in the world, there has been no object of a temporal character more desirable to me, than that of having it in my power to render to every man his due. Hence, I toiled with industry equal to my strength. I endeavored to avoid expenses; but when I had a family to provide for, this was impossible. Sickness subjected me to doctor's bills, and children were to be clothed, fed, and educated. After I went on the farm, my crops often failed, and I was never able to make any clear money by that business. Under these and other discouraging circumstances, my health gave way; and at length under the pressure of various kinds of trial, my constitution seemed to fail, and I was overtaken with the typhus fever. This disease appeared to prostrate my physical strength, and desolate the remaining powers of the nervous system. In order to raise me above the fever, recourse was had to powerful stimulants. Hence, when I felt the returns of weakness, stimulants were the only remedy within my reach; I could get hold of no other thing that would relieve me. The paroxysms of nervous disease that frequently occurred, would deprive me of the exercise of my rational understanding, and the remedy unavoidably taken was sometimes, by those who knew not the case, declared to be the disease. Hence, my moral character was called in question. Reports were spread abroad that I was become the victim of intemperance. A consequence of which was, that when I came to Philadelphia to attend the Yearly Meeting in the year 1823, a number of Friends at the close of the Meeting for sufferings on sixth day, desired me to stop with them. I did so; and they informed that reports very unfavorable to my character, were in circulation;—and therefore in their opinion I had better not attend the Yearly Meeting, but for the present return to my family.

On this afflicting occasion, the energies of my mind became prostrated, and my strength so gone from me that I returned home under deep discouragement, reflecting on my situation, and thinking I had none to look to, or to lean upon. A horror of great darkness fell upon me, and it seemed as if the lion of the forest was let loose to roar against me, and even to destroy me utterly. For a time my mind was almost distracted; and I frequently thought of putting off all dependence upon the Society of Friends, and of standing separate and alone. But when I thought of leaving the Society, this objection was always present with me: that as certainly as the children of Israel were to dwell alone, and not to mix with the surrounding nations,—so was the Society of Friends; for they were called out from among the various classes of men, and they were to stand separate, in order that the force of their example might have a proper effect upon the surrounding inhabitants. I could not therefore leave the Society; although I could feel little or no support to the mind, either inward or outward. Sometimes there would be a short interval of light and hope, but soon I would again feel lost, and left to myself.

Thus for several years, I endured a state of much suffering and various deep trials, among which was the removal of several of my children by death. I was also under the necessity of selling the farm as before noted, and thus was turned out upon the world poor, and pennyless. But the most trying of all was, that my character among Friends had become so far blasted, that it was thought proper by some to deny me the standing of a minister in the Society. I was accordingly removed from a seat in the meeting of ministers and elders. Under those circumstances, my poor soul was so far cast down, that all prospect of recovery was frequently lost: and that which gave the greatest power and force to those feelings was a consciousness that I had not kept my place, but had frequently given way to an excessive use of stimulants, in order to conquer or soothe the horror of my situation. But among all the remedies for distress, there is none more dreadful than that of intemperance. It not only fails to relieve, but it adds an incalculable amount to the affliction. No one can conceive the horror and anguish that I felt and passed through. It was a state of suffering that baffles all description; and when once a poor creature is landed in it, every step taken on that ground is making his way out more difficult.

I cannot look back to the period when my standing was called in question, without feeling the most poignant remorse, that I should have been in any degree the cause of reproach to the ever blessed Principle of Truth, of which I have made profession. But from having been brought down by an attack of typhus fever, as before mentioned, to a very low and weak state, in which for several days I had no prospect of recovery, my physician gave me both laudanum and brandy; and recommended the frequent use of the latter in my case, as indispensable to my recovery. It was during this time of weakness, and under the pressure of my difficulties and trials, that I fell into the habit of drinking brandy, and thought my condition required it. Yet I never indulged in a course of excess, because of a disposition to rebel against my good and merciful Creator; but it was occasioned by reason of an overwhelming weight of weakness, and incapacity to stand my ground.

During this time of close trial, it was vain to look for any human aid; and what added to the mass of mournful feelings and views, was the disordered state of the Society of Friends. Many of the members with whom I had formerly associated, had in my opinion departed from the principles of Friends, and taken up a determination to rule the body of the Society in their own way—even though it should prostrate the character and standing of faithful Friends who could not unite with their measures. Consequently, as I was already proscribed, I sought for no strength or comfort among this class,—and stood for a time alone. Being thus weakened, broken down and discouraged, and no associates in the Society to mingle with, I do not marvel at (though I do not approve) of some of the weaknesses into which I unhappily fell. But, adored forever be the great Shepherd and Bishop of souls;—his arm is not shortened that it can not save, nor his ear grown heavy that it cannot hear. By the blessed interference of his adorable goodness, wisdom, and power, deliverance was miraculously furnished, and a way made for me to rise again into the glorious liberty of the ever blessed Truth. This I acknowledge with gratitude to have been nothing short of a Divine work. And having witnessed that my God is indeed a God of mercy and long-suffering kindness, I am humbly bound to speak well of his excellent name, and to magnify the arm of his power. Oh! how wonderful is his loving-kindness to the children of men! When, by his Spirit my mind is opened to take a view of his marvellous kindness, long-suffering, and forbearance with transgressing mortals,—no language is sufficient to do the great subject justice. Sometimes the query arises, How is it, that he permits transgressing mortals to go on year after year, in a state of rebellion against the clear impressions of his Spirit, and lengthens out the opportunity for such to return to him, and enjoy his favor? Thus he even extends his call to the eleventh hour of the day; evidently not willing that any should perish in their sins, but that all should return, repent, and live.

In my reflections upon some of the most trying and discouraging circumstances of my life, I have been convinced that a principal cause was occasioned by my accepting of a proposal made by a liberal and wealthy friend of Philadelphia. In the preceding part of my journal, I have adverted to my being accommodated with a farm in the neighborhood of Downingtown in the year 1797. I had reason to believe that this offer was made me from the motives of kindness and good-will. But I have since believed that it would have been better for me, if I had then declined to accept it, and informed the friend, that although I was poor in the world, yet I could not doubt that if I kept faithful to my good Guide, there would be a way made for me to get along.

I now see, that, being taken from a state of poverty and placed in a condition having the appearance of wealth, I was exposed to many expenses that seemed almost unavoidably connected with my changed situation. In endeavoring to fulfill the various duties that seemed to be required of me, much of my time was occupied. I was held under appointments of society, in some of which I might not have been placed, had Friends supposed I had no time to spare; but considering my circumstances as now being easy in the world, they were influenced thereby.

From my sad experience, I am convinced that it is often dangerous or of great disadvantage, for a man to be suddenly changed from a condition of poverty to one of wealth, or even the appearance of it. Some may think by placing a religious man who is poor, in easy circumstances, that he will have the power to be more useful, and can spend more of his time and property in religious services. But, by removing him suddenly from the station in which he has been placed by Divine Providence, he may be induced by the change of his circumstances, not so deeply to feel those baptisms necessary to give his mind a full acquaintance with himself, but in some measure secretly relying on the influence of his wealth and standing in society, the perfection of his spiritual qualifications may be much injured.

Now, although from a serious recurrence to my own experience, I have been led to make these remarks, yet I have no doubt there may be many cases wherein it would be altogether right and proper for the wealthy to help the poor. We are all but stewards of the good things of this life, and there is a faithfulness in the unrighteous mammon as well as in the true and spiritual riches. See this subject treated on in Luke xvi.

In tracing over my own case, I have seriously believed that I should have escaped many a sorrowful hour, and many a mournful reflection, had I found my own way through life, and been left to struggle with the affairs of this world under the circumstances in which Providence had placed me. In the event of the loss of my apparent property, I found my standing and influence in society was greatly diminished—I was forsaken also by many who had professed to be my warm friends. But none of these things would have done me any real harm, if through all I had kept my place in the Truth.

1825, 11th. mo. 15th.—This morning it seemed to be my duty to go to Darby and attend Concord Quarterly Meeting to be held there. In great tenderness of spirit I went to the meeting.—Being sensible of the humbling presence of the Divine Being mercifully attending my poor tried mind, I implored the God of all grace to continue to be with me, so that I might never more be suffered to be left to myself; for I know that in me, that is in my flesh, there dwells no good thing. Oh! the power and the glory of that heavenly stream of gospel love, that filled my heart, and engaged me in a living testimony to his goodness: in and under which, many of the assembly were reached and with myself contrited before God. For the renewed visitation of Divine love, experienced in this meeting, my soul awfully and reverently bowed before the eternal Majesty, and I returned home with a thankful and devoted heart.

16th.—This morning, the consideration of attending Caln Quarterly Meeting presented to my mind with some weight. But having also some temporal engagements, I found it best to attend to them. To the truly religious mind, there is a depth of feeling and solicitude, when there are creditors who are uneasy, and wanting their money; and especially when the means of satisfying them are lacking. This has been my case, when I could see no way but to trust in the same blessed Power and Principle which has hitherto provided for me.

17th.—I attended our monthly meeting. In it there was a long communication; but under it there was little felt that had a tendency to quicken my mind, or to raise the Divine life into dominion. I began to fear that the cause might be in myself. But on a close search, I felt acquitted, and that my love to my heavenly Helper was steadfast.

After many trials and changes in my standing and situation, I endeavored to obtain a place of comfortable subsistence in Westchester. There I commenced conveyancing, and obtained the office of Postmaster. I had for my assistant my youngest son William; but he was taken away by death on the 7th of the 1st month, 1829.—We had had three sons and eight daughters; our two sons, Joseph and Jesse both died in the year 1827; and after William was taken, all that remained of our children, were two daughters. Thus, it has consisted with the wisdom of Divine Providence to remove by death, nine of my children. My son William was an innocent and valuable young man, and bid fair to be a support for us to lean upon in advanced life. But as he left the world in peace, and seemed to have nothing that could bind him to our earth, it was for me to be resigned.

Not many weeks after William's death, my dear wife and bosom companion was taken unwell. During the early part of the time she was wasting away, we were left in a state of greater trial than we had before known, being shifted about from place to place. At length we removed to our son-in-law, Ezra Cope's, where she was particularly under the care of her two daughters, Hannah and Lydia; and continued there until the day of her death, which occurred on the 9th of the 9th month, 1829.

Being thus stripped of a beloved companion, of most blessed mind and character, I have felt it right to give some testimony concerning her exemplary and devoted life. We entered into the solemn covenant of marriage on the 26th of the 5th month, in the year 1790, and were permitted to live together until the day of her removal by death. Having very little to begin with, our passage through the world was attended with many trials. But under all the variety of circumstances we met with, she was cheerful, and never known to murmur or complain of her situation. It was my lot frequently to leave home in the discharge of my religious duty; but I never found her to stand in my way, nor to conclude she could not get along without me. On the other hand, she held it to be her duty to make all the preparation for me in her power; and the sweet and tender regard which she manifested both when parting and meeting again, had a powerful tendency to support me under those trials. Even when we had a number of children she appeared to possess a mind settled in a confidence that there always would be a way for her to get along. When I was about to go to England and Ireland, I felt it to be a very serious trial, and that if she had said one word against my going, I should not have been able to prosecute the journey. But on this occasion I could see no difference. She had seriously weighed the concern and thought it was right for me to go, and therefore was as cheerful as on other occasions. During my absence in this journey, she became the mother of another child. This circumstance she met with fortitude and resignation; and thought she had no occasion to complain.

It was our lot to have eleven children; and for a time they appeared to be as fine and healthy children as any. But at length one of them died with the dysentery. On this occasion I had a further opportunity of witnessing her solid and passive state of mind. She did not appear to be moved from her general state of composure and quiet resignation. She afterwards saw the death of eight others of her children—and in all these cases, I did not find that she ever lost her judgment, or was in any degree disqualified for paying to them the proper and necessary attention. I remarked to her, that I was thankful to see that she was so well supported amidst all those serious trials. Her reply was, that she did not consider their deaths as an accident,—but that the removal of her children was all in wisdom, and ordered by Him who did all things for the best; and that therefore it was her duty to be resigned. And this was the cause why she was prepared to part with those dear objects of affection, without a murmur.

She was one of those excellent individuals who understood well the propriety of minding her own business, and very seldom or never was found improperly meddling with the concerns of others. She was a woman who knew what it was to have the animal passions kept in great subjection to an enlightened judgment; and having placed a just estimate on the value of this world's riches, she appeared to have no anxiety about the accumulation of wealth, either for herself or her children. In conversation, she seldom made use of many words; but her mind was cheerful and her manners were innocent and engaging.

Although she might be considered a very domestic character, yet she occasionally mingled with her neighbors and friends. It was however one of her greatest earthly comforts that her principal enjoyments were in her own family; and she believed her duties in this life consisted mainly in taking the necessary care of her household affairs, and the proper education of her children. I have often admired at the uniform obedience of every one of them to all her commands and wishes. She would sometimes say, she thought the principal duties of a mother were in her own family, especially during the minority of her children, and that she believed there was a snare in going much abroad and leaving them under care of domestics.—When she heard of mothers that would leave home for days together, and had an infant and little children that were left to be taken care of by others, she would say, their feelings must be very different from hers: for in her view women that had children were in duty bound to watch over and take proper care of them. She believed there was a possibility of getting into such a habit of going abroad and making social visits, that people would become uneasy if they stayed at home. Whereas, if they had a proper regard for their families and domestic duties, they would be much happier and more useful, to go less abroad.

She also had a testimony against talking about her neighbors to their disadvantage; saying she thought those who find little else to converse about, were not very safe or very profitable company. She considered the attendance of our religious meetings at home as a reasonable duty; but she said there were other duties to be performed that were more out of sight, and that the nearer she kept to what was right in the fulfillment of all her duties, the less difficulty she found in keeping the mind right when at meetings.

My trials and disappointments in my temporal concerns had been many and grievous. But although we were almost turned out upon the world empty-handed, she never murmured, nor reflected on me; but endeavored to keep me from every thing like despair. The happy state of resignation to the precious gift of God in herself, in which she lived, gave her a firmness of mind that no adversity of circumstances could move or unsettle.

I attended upon her during her last sickness and at her death: and was furnished with evidences that did more in confirming my mind in the great doctrine of immortality and eternal life, than any other opportunity I had ever before witnessed. In her there was a uniform confidence in the goodness and mercy of God, that never forsook her. One very important trait in her character was, that she did not wish to know any thing before the right time. She remarked to me, that she believed it was possible even for very goodly kind of people, to want to know more of futurity than it was consistent with Infinite Wisdom to permit. Believing as she did in the immortality of the soul, she was confident that the condition of it in eternity would be as perfect as it was capable of being—and therefore on this subject, she knew that it would be wrong to indulge any anxiety about it. In this calm and dignified state of mind she continued, and always apparently contented. Thus she observed the gradual wasting and decay of her bodily powers, without any apparent anxiety.

During the last two weeks of her life, it was her practice to retire to bed about nine o'clock in the evening; and she preferred my taking care of her through the night. She generally slept till between twelve and one o'clock. Then waking up, she took some refreshment, and something to allay her cough—after which she would converse pleasantly on the various occurrences that we had known together—so interesting were her remarks and her cheerful converse that morning would often come before I was aware. At length the morning came when she said to me, "My dear, I have now passed through the last night." And so it proved. In the afternoon she requested me to place her as upright in the bed as I could. She then took a farewell look of a friend who stood at the foot of the bed. She next turned her eyes upon her two daughters who were at its side. After looking at them for some time, she turned her countenance upon me and with an affection that language cannot describe, continued to view me for some time. Then, closing her eyes, she remained perfectly still, and departed with such quietude that I could not discern the moment of her ceasing to breathe. But before she left us, she told us her day's work was done, and that she was going in peace.

After the decease of my companion, being invited to the city of Philadelphia by some of my acquaintance, I went there, and commenced a small tea store. But a few months convinced me that I could not stand upon any thing like a reasonably independent footing there. After weighing things in my own mind, I felt that I might retire, and endeavor to gain such a state of inward confidence and quietude, as appeared to me particularly desirable in advanced life. I accordingly left the city and returned to Chester county, where the time passed pleasantly along without my being much engaged in any way.

1832, 11th mo. 20th.—I am now in the habitation of my kind friends, Mordecai Hayes and wife, who have generously accommodated me with a comfortable home. Being therefore free from all worldly cares, an opportunity was furnished to consider what may be the duties to be fulfilled in the evening of life.

This day I attended the Western Quarterly Meeting, which proved to be a time of deep suffering without any way opening for my being relieved. According to my feelings, the members of Society in this place are in a weak state, and it is not unlikely that it may not be long before some painful circumstances will occur among them. In the course of the proceedings of this

Quarterly Meeting, I perceived there were those that would be likely to sow the seeds of discord, and thus produce further cause of trial and suffering to the living and upright.

Reflecting upon the subject of the ministry among us, and the solemnity which should always attend a living gospel exercise of it, I am convinced that we have appearances in that weighty work which have not the baptizing power of Truth attending them. Such communications always have a tendency to lessen the character of preaching. It would be much better if the meetings of Friends were held in silence, than to be burdened with lifeless communications. It is truly to be desired that Friends may never become ashamed of their silent meetings, and spiritual worship. In such opportunities of solemn silence, the sincere mind may witness a deepening in the root of Divine life.

I am often deeply impressed with considerations on the awful nature of the change that is every day drawing nearer and nearer. And although, on looking back over many years of my life, I may say that much of my time has been devoted to the great cause of universal righteousness: yet I am very sensible that during part of the time I have justly been numbered among the weak members of the church. But at no time since I have been concerned for the cause of Truth, has my soul wilfully turned away from my God to follow other beloveds, however in some things I have wandered from the true ground of safety, by endeavoring to obtain relief to a weak tabernacle through wrong means. But through the ever adorable mercy of the Almighty, I have been tenderly cared for, and helped over all my trials and sufferings, for which I have great cause to worship and to praise his ever excellent name. While I am sensible that I am deeply indebted to Divine Goodness for his many favors and blessings from my childhood up, yet I feel that there is a constant necessity for great watchfulness, and care, lest I should fail to inherit the promises.

About the beginning of the year 1833, I attended a meeting at Center, and found my way open to deliver a clear and living testimony to the simplicity and purity of the gospel spirit; and to declare my belief that at this day it is powerfully operating upon the souls of many people; and that the great Father of mankind by his spirit is gathering home to himself sons and daughters from among all the families of the earth. It was a comfortable view in which I had to rejoice, and in thankfulness of heart reverently to worship, praise, and adore the blessed Giver of every good and perfect gift. Friends were also seriously exhorted to mind their calling; and by improving their time and talents, thus become prepared for the awful change that awaits us all; remembering the apostolic counsel to use "all diligence to make their calling and election sure, before they go hence and are seen of men no more."

I also attended Kennett Monthly Meeting, held at Marlborough. In this opportunity my mind was largely opened in a stream of gospel love, and much important matter flowed to those present. To one state I was led to speak with great solemnity; under an impression that the time was near a close with the individual, and the work behindhand; and that if the present invitation of Divine grace was not embraced there might never be another call extended. The youth were also tenderly urged to turn their backs upon the pomps and vanities of this wicked world, and all the sinful lusts of the flesh; that so the precious talents they received might be occupied and improved to the honor and glory of the great Giver, and to their everlasting peace and comfort.

In the 4th month, 1834, I attended our Yearly Meeting, held in Philadelphia. At the opening of one of the sittings it came before me to remark, that I took it for granted that we were not assembled to do our own, but the Lord's work. Hence, it was necessary that we should individually learn practically to understand the sublime testimony of one of the Lord's prophets, where he says, "Unto us a child is born,—unto us a son is given, and upon his shoulders the government shall rest." I further remarked that it was only as we came to understand his government, that we knew him to be the wonderful Counsellor,—the mighty God,—the everlasting Father, and Prince of Peace. I could say from my own experience, that as I was careful to wait in the life and power of the Divine gift,—way was made to know what to do, and what to leave undone; and, indeed, that every communication called for by the light and spirit of Truth, had the baptizing power of Truth to witness to its heavenly nature;—and pure, evangelical peace flowed as a consequence.

During the course of this Yearly Meeting, I felt my mind much impressed with a strong persuasion that there was a great want of deep inward retirement, and humble waiting upon the Head of the Church of Christ, that we might witness the government to rest upon his shoulders, and know his blessed light to enlighten us, and to furnish sound judgment on all the cases and subjects brought before us.

About the middle of the week, in the evening, I had a solemn and blessed meeting with a large number of the colored people, in their meeting house on Lombard street. The company sat in great stillness and quietude, and the time did not seem tedious to them.

On fourth day morning I was at Green street meeting, which was large, and in the early part it seemed to be very solemn: but I thought much of this solemnity was lost before it closed. This appeared to me to be the consequence of too much preaching. There were a number who spoke before me, and six after I sat down. In the afternoon, John Livingston, a Friend from Baltimore, opened and spread before the Yearly Meeting some very interesting remarks on the great subject of education. He stated that it began with our beginning, and ended only with our lives—that from the cradle to the grave we were learning. Our first impressions were received in the nursery, and all the subsequent events that we met with, had their influence in forming our characters. Hence, the importance of being taught an early subjection of our wills, so that the rational powers might be kept free, and all improper prejudices avoided. By having our minds and habits rightly formed and disciplined to the cross of Christ, we became fitted for taking a useful part in the great concerns of the church. He also held up the view that just in the same proportion as the whole system of our education was governed by the perfect principle of Truth, we were rendered and made up a body competent to the fulfillment of the duties of our time. On closing his remarks it was evident that "words fitly spoken had a powerful effect."

The 26th of the 1st month, 1835, I set out on a visit to the meetings composing Abington and Bucks Quarters. In the evening I arrived at Philadelphia where I was met by Samuel West, who was to accompany me in the journey

28th.—Had an appointed meeting at Byberry, which was large. In this opportunity, I was led to speak of the state of the ministry, and particularly to urge the necessity there was for those who thought they were called to this weighty service, to mind the right time to close,—and not continue speaking until all were wishing them to sit down. It was also observed as a painful circumstance to the hearers, when a minister continued speaking and there was no life nor power attending;—and if a Friend should, in this or any other respect, give occasion of concern, it was always right to stand open to the counsel of those who should be so kind as to speak to him on account of his mistakes. And it was further remarked, that any one who should appear to be hurt or offended because he was spoken to by a friend, could not be on sound and safe ground. This meeting ended much to my satisfaction; and we rode to Isaac Parry's the afternoon following.

29th.—Had a meeting at Horsham, in which my mind was much exercised, from a sense that the pure gift of God's spirit was not submitted to as should have been the case by some who knew the precious influence of it. Next day we had a large and blessed meet ing at Plymouth. The great and important work of man's redemption and salvation, was livingly and powerfully illustrated. The solemnity that was felt gave ample evidence that the minds of many present were deeply impressed with the importance of the testimony.

31st.—At a meeting at Upper Dublin, I felt much on account of a spirit of unbelief in the Divine gift to man. It came before me to show that every man stood in need of a guide to conduct him safely through time; that those who accepted the *reason* of man, as this all sufficient guide,—must be mistaken, because it was not capable of looking into the future: but this, a competent guide should do. Many other proofs occurred at the time, going to show that the doctrines of a divine revelation, was the only rational doctrine on which to place our unlimited confidence, as a safe guide to conduct us through all the trials and difficulties of life. The meeting ended with much solemnity. After dining at Spencer Thomas's, we rode to James Paul's and lodged. Next day, we attended Abington meeting, and had a large and very interesting meeting at Frankford, at three o'clock in the afternoon. In this opportunity my mind was opened into some very clear views of the work of man's redemption:—showing that it consisted of a full and perfect submission of the animal spirit in man, to the light and power of "the word of God;"—and that those who had experience of this found indeed that "the word of God is quick and powerful—dividing asunder between soul and spirit." That is, the soul being set at liberty from the state of thraldom, in which it had been held, as the consequence of living "after the flesh,"—had the opportunity given to it to rule and govern the lower nature in man; and thus attained to a state of perfect freedom. But if, when it was thus visited and aided, it chose to return to the fleshy desires and inclinations,—it thus became again plunged into bondage; and, by living after the flesh, it must die to all the heavenly and spiritual powers, and be lost in the vortex of sin and misery. The meeting was a favored one, and closed in the life. After which we rode to Thornton Walton's and lodged.

2d mo. 2.—Had a meeting at Bustleton, under some disadvantages for want of better accommodations; but, keeping patiently to the openings before me, had the satisfaction to witness a blessed solemnity together. After this I attended Abington Quarterly Meeting, and had a meeting at the Billet, or Hatborough, on sixth day. On seventh day had a meeting at Montgomery Square; in which I felt engaged to show, that as the great business of man's salvation was purely spiritual, it was impossible for outward or elementary means to accomplish the work. Hence, water baptism and all other material dependencies were rejected. The meeting ended under a satisfactory feeling of solemnity, and I retired to the habitation of our friend Joseph Foulke with a thankful heart.

8th.—We were at Gwynedd meeting; in which I felt my mind extremely barren and poor. But by waiting in spirit upon the great Helper of His people, way opened to become clear in a testimony to the value of the "unspeakable gift." In the afternoon we rode to Norristown, where a large gathering of people assembled, and I had an open and blessed opportunity. Much solemnity prevailed, and it appeared that many minds were reached. Next day we had a meeting at Providence, which, though small, was a comfortable season. A number of the Seventh Day Baptists were present, and requested that I would have a meeting with them. On consideration, I felt easy to accede to the proposal, and the day following had a solid and instructive opportunity with them. Thence we rode to John Foulke's, at Richland.

12th.—Attended Richland meeting, which ended with a satisfactory evidence that we had been favored together. On sixth day we rode to Allentown, and had a very interesting meeting there. Many present seemed to be brought to a state of serious reflection, and much solemnity covered the assembly. The next day we had a blessed meeting at Easton. In this opportunity I found the way open to show the nature of the great work of redemption. When the meeting closed, we had cause to admire the goodness of our holy Helper in condescending to be both mouth and wisdom, tongue and utterance. In opening the doctrines which came before me, I was particularly led to show, that the sons of the morning did speak only the things that they knew; and that Paul was taught the doctrine which he preached by revelation only.

16th.—Had a meeting at Plumstead in the morning, and another in the evening at Doylestown. Both of these were solid and edifying opportunities. In the afternoon of the day following I had a religious opportunity with the children of Martha Hampton's school; and lodged at John Watson's. Next day attended Buckingham meeting, and I found it to be a laborious opportunity. The weight of my concern was principally toward those who had been visited with the day-spring from on high,—but who had not been faithful to the light with which they had been blessed. In their case I was led into much serious expostulation, and had a hope that the labor would not be lost. But the meeting was closed, as I thought, too soon. It felt to me as if more time ought to have been spent in a retired state—but, closing as it did, the true point of solemnity was not gained.

19th.—I was at Solebury meeting; wherein my mind was opened into a clear view of the work of man's salvation; and the testimony delivered had a solemnizing effect. In the evening I attended a large gathering at New Hope. In this opportunity my mind was opened in a remarkable manner, in explanation of the great work of the salvation of the soul of man. When I had closed, a young woman arose and proceeded at considerable length; but it was evident that the solemnity was leaving the meeting. I felt very tender of the young woman, and was much tried with the circumstance. At length, I spoke to her, and desired that she would try to come to a close;—mentioning that it was a serious thing to disturb the solemnity of the meeting. She tried to go on, but found she could not, and therefore sat down.

On the 20th, I had a large and laborious meeting at Wrightstown, in this opportunity I was led to show that all gospel-ministry was the fruit of the Divine power and wisdom,—and that no human acquirements can ever produce a single gospel minister. It was a blessed meeting; but on recurring to my feelings there, I am still impressed with sadness. Although I was led to speak on the subject of the ministry with great plainness, yet it seemed to me as though the proper effect of the concern was not produced. But this must be left: and a kind of preaching may continue to be suffered, which is out of the pure guidance of the Divine Spirit

Next day, had a meeting at Makefield. It was large, and in it the doctrine of Divine revelation was opened, and shown to be the true and only principle upon which the true church has always been grounded and built. It was a satisfactory meeting, and ended well. In the afternoon, we rode to Newtown and lodged at Joseph Briggs'. Here we had the company of our kind friend, Edward Hicks. During the evening our conversation was interesting, embracing some of the leading doctrines of Christianity, in which we could see eye to eye.

22d.—Attended Newtown meeting, where I found the way open to deliver a plain testimony to the power and wisdom of the "unspeakable gift" to man. My confidence was renewed in the universal operation of this Divine Spirit. It appeared to me that in the progress of this principle, many would be gathered from off the mountains of an empty profession, to the living experience of the power and government of the ever-blessed Spirit of Truth. Next day I was at a meeting at the Falls; and therein felt my mind opened into a general view of the nature of man, and of the great work of his redemption from under the influence and power of his own animal spirit:—showing that this could only be perfected by the aid of the word or spirit of God. The testimony appeared to have a deep and solemn effect upon the minds of many present. After sitting down a short time, I felt a weight of concern to hold up to the view of the mothers present, the vast importance of the duties to which they were called in regard to their tender offspring;—showing that as they had the opportunity of making the first impressions upon them, it was of great consequence that they should make no other than correct impressions upon their tender minds. In the conclusion of this meeting, I felt thankful for the aid that I experienced in discharging my duty among the people.

On the 24th, had a meeting at Middletown, which ended in the life. The next day I attended the Quarterly Meeting of Ministers and Elders, at Wrightstown, and the day following that, for business; both of which were satisfactory to me. The 27th, had a meeting at Pennsbury, and in the evening had a large and interesting meeting at Bristol. The doctrine delivered in this opportunity appeared to make a deep impression. After I sat down, a short but lively testimony was borne in concurrence with what had been delivered. The meeting then sat for some time in a satisfactory, solemn silence.

On first day the 1st of 3d month, in the morning, attended Byberry meeting in company with George Hatton. In the afternoon was at Holmesburg. Our meeting at this place was much crowded, and many had to stand; yet there was no disposition to move until the close. I had great occasion thankfully to adore the great Shepherd of the sheep, for the abundant aid furnished in this memorable meeting. It was a season in which I was led to point out the nature of the operation of the all-powerful gift of God to man, and particularly to dwell upon the vast importance of the redemption of the soul from under the influence of the natural or animal spirit. It appeared to me, that in the doctrine which Paul preached, he had the same view of the nature of the saving power of the word of God, that I was led to open to that assembly. As this meeting was chiefly composed of other societies. I was also led to remark, that as the glorious light of Truth opened upon the minds of the people, women would come forth in the ministry, as they had done in the primitive church;—that the religious rights and privileges of females had been acknowledged only where the true doctrines of the gospel have been embraced,—these privileges being best understood by those who best understand the gospel spirit.

This meeting was the closing of my public labors in this journey. On looking back calmly over the visit, and taking a retrospective view of the meetings I have attended, I think I may say that in almost, if not quite every instance I have witnessed the most powerful ability furnished that I have ever experienced at any time of my life. Nor do I think that I ever before knew more of the sympathy and unity of my friends. I have therefore cause to say, "Return, O my soul, to the place of thy rest, for the Lord hath dealt bountifully with thee."

The following letter, having reference to the preceding journey, may be properly introduced here. It was dated 9th of 3d mo., 1835.

"Dear Friend:—I have several times since my return home recurred to thy request that I would write to thee. After I had gone through my visit and retired from the field of action, it seemed as though I was unfit for anything but to be retired and quiet. And this continues to be much the state in which I am landed. I may say, however, that at no time of my life have I felt a stronger solicitude, that the pure principles and doctrines of the Christian religion might be rightly understood and honestly embraced, than since I have been released from the late arduous journey.

Were this the case the world over, the human family would feel that they were all one happy brotherhood; and kindness and harmony would reign from sea to sea, and from the rivers to the ends of the earth. Convinced I am, that all which has yet been known of the brightness and glory of God's redeeming power, would be but as the twilight of morning compared with a meridian sun. Yes, my dear friend, if the souls of mankind were emancipated from the miserable dominion of the animal spirit, and perfectly united with the Word of life, a new order of things would be introduced. Instead of being bound down by pride and prejudice, every faculty would be brought to the clearness of the light of Truth; and all the creation of God would be seen as the product of unlimited power and wisdom. In this heavenly enjoyment of the blessed works of Omnipotence, being ourselves a part of the same, we should freely admit, that the one-half had never been told us of the perfection of his order and government.

To see my fellow creatures muddling along in this world, the slaves of every passion, and blindly expecting to improve their happiness by heaping up the treasures of the earth,—is a circumstance which sometimes almost overpowers every faculty, and I feel as if I could say to my great and benevolent Creator, How long, O thou of infinite power and majesty, wilt thou suffer thy erring and transgressing creatures thus to put darkness for light,—evil for good, and misery for happiness! Shall the human family, who are the declared objects of thy redeeming love, never rise above their present corrupted and sorrowful condition? Yes, my dear friend, the great Shepherd of the sheep is doubtless secretly and powerfully acting his own blessed part;—and many shall come from the east and from the west, from the north and from the south, and sit down with his gathered host in the heavenly kingdom.

But it seems to me, that in aid of this glorious work, the time is coming when the female part of society will be brought out into the exercise of the pure and glorious gift, to the edification and comfort of the lambs of the flock. I think too, that I can see in the all-powerful progress of the Holy Spirit, there will be a still more effectual shaking of all formal professors and professions,—that those who have been attempting to promote the Lord's work in their own will and wisdom, will be removed out of the way,—and all that tends to darken the counsel of God in the souls of the people, and to lead to a dependence upon outward and elementary means, will be understood to number among the ministers of anti-Christ.

Having this faith I feel abundantly convinced that the society of Friends are in a very responsible station. We have been brought to a more full and clear profession of a belief in the inward revelation of God to the souls of men, than any other class of Christian professors. Hence, it must be expected that we should demonstrate the correctness of our principles by our practice. But if on the contrary, we should show to others, that with all this profession we are living in the gratification of the carnal mind, and are fulfilling the lusts of the flesh,—it may be said to us, You of all the families of the earth have I known, and you will I punish.

But, my dear friend, from what I have seen and felt, I cannot think otherwise than that an important body are coming forth from among our beloved young people, who, seeing the beauty and excellency of the Christian path, will be in earnest to walk in it. I am, however, often concerned for these, lest they should be led off by false lights and visionary opinions. If they were brought to understand that the great work of the soul's redemption can only be perfected by yielding obedience to the Holy Spirit, and that it is the teaching of this Spirit which calls us to stand separate from the improper indulgence of the animal spirit,—they would soon see into the glorious consequence of their obedience to all its impressions and calls of duty.

I have also been led, in my retired moments, to admire the clear and perfect understanding which our worthy predecessors had, of the nature of the gospel dispensation. We find them coming out from under a formal ministry, and bearing a faithful testimony against it. They fully believed, that all true ministry was the fruit of the divine gift of God to man; and that, as this gift was freely given, so those who received it were freely to minister, as they should be led by it. But they were aware, that no man could command the movements of this divine and all-sufficient principle. They that were furnished with it, were to wait upon it, and minister only when and as they should be thereunto moved by it. Hence, they were led to sit down together in silence, that they might wait upon God to put them forth, and not run or speak in their own wills. This state of silent waiting was found to be profitable for every one to enter into, because therein every individual was furnished with an opportunity secretly to worship God in the spirit, according to the qualification received of him at the time. Our predecessors also were enlightened to see, that *prayer*, in order to be acceptable to God, must be dictated by his own blessed spirit immediately moving thereunto. Hence all those forms of prayer which were commonly used among other professors, were to them little better than mere idolatry. So also in regard to the custom of singing. They could not believe that the matter expressed with a musical tone of the voice, was rendered any more acceptable to God from the mere sound of words so modulated; and therefore they rejected all those outward forms of music and singing in their solemn meetings; preferring a silent introversion of mind in sincerity of heart, and an inward spiritual devotion,—to all outward and formal acts. Not only as related to their solemn meetings, did they leave the customs of other professors; but when these called the scriptures the word of God, and held it as their belief that none could be saved unless they were furnished with the book,—Friends knew and declared that the scriptures taught very different doctrines. Indeed it is admirable with what clearness their minds were opened on all important subjects; so that they seemed to be alive to everything that militated against the advancement of the pure and righteous principles and testimonies of the gospel of Christ. Trusting in and following the same holy guide, I am persuaded that we of the present time, may in like manner perform the work of our day. JESSE KERSEY."

On seventh day the 11th of 4th month, 1835, I attended the Yearly Meeting of Ministers and Elders, at Philadelphia. It was, in the morning, a meeting of some comfort, and light seemed to shine upon it. In the afternoon Elisha Dawson laid before us his concern to visit some parts of Europe, which was generally united with.

Next day I attended the meeting at Cherry street. It was a very crowded assembly, and in it my mind was opened in a view of the nature of the gospel ministry; as also into some very clear ideas of the way and work of man's redemption.

The 19th of the 10th month, 1835, I left home in company with Isaac Haynes in order to visit Friends at their Yearly Meeting in Baltimore, on the way we attended West Nottingham meeting which was small; also had a satisfactory opportunity with the inhabitants at Conewingo Bridge. Thence we proceeded on to Baltimore and lodged at Enoch Clapp's. On first day, the 25th, I was at a meeting on Lombard street. In this opportunity I was led to show the agreement in the doctrine of the Savior and the apostle Paul, his minister to the gentiles.

In attending the several sittings of the Yearly Meeting, I thought they were favored opportunities. At the close, I had an evening meeting, which was a blessed season of favor. On my way homewards, I was present at meetings at Little Falls and Deer Creek, to my satisfaction—the latter was a blessed and heavenly meeting.

On the 19th of the 8th month, 1836, I left my home and rode to Darby, where I lodged at the house of my old friends, John and Rachel Hunt. They are both advanced in life, but are warm in their love to Friends, and they possess clear and intelligent minds. Next day I went to the city, and spent the evening in the company of the widow and children of my late friend, doctor John Moore.

In looking at the prospect of religious service now before me, I have been brought into deep feeling, and very sensibly impressed with a conviction of my incapacity (as a man) for the undertaking. But, believing that I am called, now in advanced life, to make this sacrifice, I humbly hope that as my mind is centred in the great Head of the church, I may be helped through; so as in no instance to dishonor the great cause of Truth. In considering the obligations that I am under to the bountiful Giver of every good and perfect gift, I have thought they are indeed truly great; and it is my sincere desire now in the evening of life, to follow with integrity every opening of duty clearly pointed out, that so the work of my day may be honestly and faithfully performed.

21st.—I have attended three meetings to-day. In that held at Cherry street in the morning, I felt the way open to deliver a short testimony to the power and certainty of the gift of the spirit. At the close of this opportunity, my mind was deeply affected, under a sense of the weakness which was felt in consequence of a multitude of words, without the baptizing power of Truth being witnessed to reign over all.

In the evening, I was again tried with two long sermons that left me very poor and in suffering. I have said in my heart, gracious God, how is it that thy poor servant should be thus stripped, and left as it were under the power of death itself! Surely, there must be a cause: and if it is in me, oh! help me to do all that is necessary, for its removal. And now, as I am going out in thy service, grant, O Lord, that my eyes and my understanding may be kept open;—so that I may see and know all that is required,—and *that* do, and no more. Let not thy servant fall into the mistake of attempting to minister, to gratify the ears of the people. Oh! preserve me in the life and light of thy own blessed Spirit;—that so, all that I may say or do, may be to thy honor, and that all my selfish nature may be laid in the dust. For thine is the power and the glory, and the honor of all thy own great and blessed works, —and to us belongs nothing but blushing and confusion of face.

From Philadelphia, I went to the house of my kind friend Joseph Briggs, at Newtown, Bucks county. Poverty of spirit was my attendant, nor could I, for a season, feel as if I was competent for anything. It seemed as though there was not anything for me to rejoice in or to be glad about. I know it is a great attainment in all conditions to be contented. The apostle Paul knew what it was to suffer want, and also to abound; and he had gained the ground of content, both in poverty and when he abounded. If this happy state can be gained by one, then surely it may be by another. To be able to endure all things, and keep the everlasting patience, is very desirable. By cherishing a state of resignation, much may be done; and without it all that we can have is of but little value.

While I was at Newtown, I felt the way open to attend Burlington Quarterly Meeting, held at Mount Holly. On getting into the town I thought it right to appoint a meeting with the inhabitants generally: and accordingly it was held, and proved to be a solemn and blessed opportunity. The Quarterly Meeting was also satisfactory: but a proposal to open the shutters near the close was trying to me, and I excused myself and withdrew. The meeting had been furnished with extensive communication before, and it seemed to me out of time to attempt anything more at that period. After returning to Newtown, I made ready to prosecute my journey to New York State; and on 2d day the 6th of 9th month, I arrived in the city of New York, in the evening.

On fifth day, I attended Purchase Monthly Meeting, and the next day, that at Shapaqua, which was a precious opportunity. In the afternoon I made a visit to William Carpenter, who appeared to be fast going to the house appointed for all the living. The evening was passed in pleasant and instructive conversation at the house of Samuel Sutton where we lodged.

On sixth day, the 9th, I was at Croton meeting, where qualification was furnished to deliver a clear and plain testimony to the pure and unchangeable Truth. Next day had a meeting at Salem.

On first day the 18th, I was at Saratoga meeting, which was an instructive opportunity. The subject of communication was the great mercy of God in granting to his rational creation the gift of his holy spirit.

On fifth day the 22d, I was at Pittstown meeting, which was small. In the afternoon we returned to Troy, and I felt my mind released, with a comfortable evidence that I might return from these northern parts. Next day we came to Albany; and I attended the meeting of Friends, but found a concern to have an appointed meeting there in the evening: which was a satisfactory season. After this we went back to Troy, and after attending the funeral of Robert Barton, had an evening meeting there.

Notwithstanding much poverty of spirit was my attendant in this journey, yet I have been helped through much to my own comfort and relief; and have great cause humbly to admire the mercy and goodness of the great Shepherd of his flock.

During this journey it was remarkable to me to find my way was generally very open: and though some of the meetings were small, they were all instructive and blessed opportunities.

After my return home, a concern arose to visit some meetings, appoint some, westward, as far as Huntington. I set out in company with Charles Buffington, and had an interesting meeting at Strasburg; thence to Lampeter—and one at a house intended for general use, about eight miles northward. Thence to Lancaster, Yorktown, Newberry, Lisborn, and Lewisburg, where I had meetings to the relief of my own mind. We then rode to Warrington and were entertained at John Walter's. The meeting at Warrington seemed like a poor concern: but at Huntington, we had a large and interesting meeting. During our stay here, we lodged at Joel Garretson's. At a village called Petersburg, I had a large and blessed opportunity, and another at a place called Berlin. Thence we returned to Yorktown and had an evening meeting, in which way opened to hold up to view the difference between a mere formal profession of religion, and a living experience of its redeeming effects.

On the 5th of the 8th month, 1837, I went to Philadelphia in order to attend the Quarterly Meeting there, and appoint some meetings, as way might open. On first day morning we had a solid and instructive meeting at Cherry street. In the evening, my mind was livingly opened in the pure stream of the blessed gospel of Christ; and it appeared to me that many present were brought under the baptizing power of the spirit of Truth. Great solemnity prevailed, and the meeting ended in a very satisfactory manner. Next day, in the Quarterly Meeting of Ministers and Elders, I was thankful to feel my mind calm and peaceful; and it was no small satisfaction to meet with a number of Friends from different parts of the country. I also had a meeting at Green street, which was one of those blessed opportunities in which the power of Truth was felt to be in dominion. On third-day evening I had another favored meeting at Spruce street.

During the time spent in Philadelphia, my mind was led to take a view of the condition of many Friends in that place; and it appeared to me that it was far from being a desirable one to a sincere humble-minded man. Their children are much exposed to many dangers and temptations—and many of the heads of families, having to gain the means of subsistence by trade and commerce, are often involved in great trials from the changes and fluctuations that are frequently taking place. They do not therefore enjoy that quietude of mind, and exemption from many difficulties, which is or may be attained in a way of living attended with fewer wants and less exposure to temptations. Hence, I have become persuaded, that it is often a great mistake on the part of those who are brought up in the simplicity of a country life,—to change their residence and remove into these large cities, more especially when they engage largely in those kinds of business with which they are little or not at all acquainted. Indeed, it is very doubtful whether any one entering largely into business, can go through with all that (in the present mode of doing things) seems in some sort necessary to be done in conducting business in the city, without more or less swerving from correct principles, and departing from the duty of doing to others as they would be done by.

9th.—I left the city and went to Darby, where I was kindly accommodated at the house of my old friend Rachel Hunt. On first day I attended Darby meeting, which did not seem to me to be so lively as it had been in former days;—several of the old and valuable members having been removed by death. On second and third days, I was at the Quarterly Meeting held at Concord. The opportunity was one of much solemnity, in which I had an open time, and the meeting appeared to be a profitable and instructive season.

On fifth day the 17th, I was at an appointed meeting at Kennett. Here I was led to show that Christianity was not only a religion of Divine origin, but that it was also a religion of universal application. But if the formalities that priestcraft had attached to it, were to be credited, this would destroy the universality of its character. But the blessed Jesus had declared that we were not to follow any of the lo heres, or lo theres; because the kingdom of heaven was within. It was evident also, that our early Friends maintained this view, and wisely rejected all external ceremonies,—declaring that the grace of God (which, according to the testimony of Paul, was universally bestowed) was an all-sufficient means of salvation; and therefore no other means were necessary. This doctrine they have handed down to us, free from all mistake or difficulty,—uniting as they did with all the apostles and primitive believers, in maintaining the sublimity and dignity of the blessed gospel that is preached in every creature.

After this meeting, in company with doctor Rolf C. Marsh, I went to Moses Pennock's and lodged; and on sixth day had a large and instructive meeting at Kennet-Square. It was cause of gratitude to find in this opportunity the blessed presence of Him who promised to be to his dedicated children both mouth and wisdom, tongue and utterance. From this meeting I was kindly conveyed to Thomas Ellicott's, where I spent the time agreeably; and on first day the 20th, was at New Garden meeting in the forenoon,—and paid a visit to George Gawthrop's family in the afternoon. Next day I was at the Western Quarterly Meeting of Ministers and Elders, and the day following I attended the general meeting for business. It was a very large gathering; but it seemed to be my place to be silent. In the afternoon I went to Caln, and attended the Quarterly Meeting there on fourth and fifth days. After the close of the meeting I returned home.

On seventh day the 26th, in company with Abner Chalfant, I went to Wilmington, and the next day I was at meeting with Friends there, near the close of which I had a short testimony to deliver.

It has been remarkable to me, that of latter time, in almost all the instances in which I have been engaged in public testimony, I have felt bound to advocate the doctrine of a measure of the Divine Spirit being given to every man to profit withal,—and to show that, according to the scriptures, this gift is universal; and therefore the means of salvation is not confined to any sect, nation, or party. By the power of this gift, the innumerable company which John saw, were gathered out of every nation, kindred, tongue and people.

Hence it is evident that the religion of the Son of

God is of universal application. But if the grace or spirit of God was not sufficient, then this religion would not be universal, and of course it could not be held to be of Divine origin. To support the doctrine of the universality of Christianity we must strip it of all the dead formalities that have been unwisely heaped upon it. This our early Friends were zealous to do, leaving us an example that we should follow their footsteps.

At half-past seven o'clock in the evening, I met an interesting company of people near the Brandywine mills. In this meeting my mind was opened into a view of the freedom which is gained by coming into a state of perfect conformity to the great principle of Truth. It was clear to me that there could be no other way or means by which the prejudices could ever be subdued. Hence, we have cause to admire the goodness of God, in giving to his creature man this "unspeakable gift." If we were deprived of the aid of this important Guide, there would be nothing left by which the great family of mankind could ever be gathered into the kingdom of heaven. Indeed, our union with God, as well as our redemption from evil, can only be perfected by the power of this precious gift.

28th.—Having felt my mind drawn in the love of the gospel, to visit the inhabitants of Newcastle, we rode there and made known our prospect. A meeting was appointed to come together at half-past six o'clock in the evening: about which time we went to the court-house, and remained there about three-quarters of an hour; but finding few persons attend, the meeting was closed, and I came away satisfied. Having done what I could, I felt that for the present I was clear. The next evening, I had an interesting meeting at

Wilmington. On this occasion as heretofore, I had to maintain the doctrine of a divine gift to man, and to show that if this doctrine was departed from, there was nothing permanent and certain left for the mind to rest upon.

On the 30th, I had a very satisfactory meeting near Naaman's Creek, and was kindly accommodated at the house of Joseph Baynes, an English Friend. In the evening of next day, I had a meeting about four miles from Wilmington on the way toward Philadelphia. It was a solid and instructive opportunity, in which I had to open to the people the nature of man's redemption and salvation. I was also led to request the assembly to read the instructions of Christ to his disciples on the great subject of prayer.

On the 3d of the 9th month, I attended Chichester meeting, and in the evening, had a large meeting at Old Chester. Both those meetings were solemn and blessed opportunities; in which my mind was opened into a full and perfect view of the universality of the gift of God to man,—showing that the religion of Jesus Christ must necessarily be free from all the formalities that ignorance and priestcraft have imposed upon it. Of this the proof had been given by the Son of God himself, when he forewarned his disciples and followers that many would come in his name, saying, Lo here! and Lo there is Christ; but, said he, "go ye not after them,"—for "the kingdom of heaven is within you." Now it must be evident that every Lo here, and Lo there has an outward and external relation, and cannot lead the mind to that inward fountain of Light and Life which is the consolation of the children of God.

The principal amount of my labors in the gospel in this journey thus far, has been to hold up among the people the *certainty* of a spiritual Guide to man. In this I have been much assisted by the plain testimonies of the scriptures that have been brought to my remembrance on the subject. They abundantly prove the truth of this doctrine. An unusual quiet has remarkably prevailed in all the meetings that I have had in this journey; and I have found my good and gracious God to be a present help in every needful time. He has been to me mouth and wisdom, tongue and utterance. To him alone be all the glory of his own blessed work. I am fully persuaded that it is his good pleasure to gather all into his holy enclosure who are willing to come to him and to be governed by his pure and holy spirit.

After this, I again attended the meeting at Old Chester, and was renewedly convinced of the necessity there was for Friends when they meet for the professed purpose of divine worship, to keep alive in a state of honest and faithful waiting on God, in order to be strengthened and edified together. In the afternoon a larger meeting came together, in which life was felt to be in dominion, and the opportunity was satisfactory. In this meeting I was led to hold up a view of the simplicity and excellency of the religion of Christ, and that its fundamental duties could be understood by every rational being. I was also fully convinced if mankind would everywhere strip the profession and promulgation of it from all monied and selfish considerations, we should soon find that all the formal obligations now contended for, would be let fall, and the common mind would centre in a full conviction that the blessed gift of the Spirit or Light of Christ within, diligently attended to and obeyed, was all that is necessary in the work of man's redemption and salvation.

12th.—I had a large and very respectable meeting in a house belonging to the Baptists. After this opportunity closed, I felt thankful, because I had a comfortable evidence that all was well concluded.

It has appeared to me a melancholy circumstance that any who once knew the principles professed by our early Friends, should, like the Galatians, go back again to the weak and beggarly elements, and thus mar the great work of universal righteousness in the earth.

14th.—I had a large and solemn meeting not far from the Seven Stars tavern. In this opportunity my mind was livingly opened in the clearness and power of the ever-blessed gospel; and it appeared that many present were brought under feelings of great solemnity. I was particularly led to open the station of man in the creation, according to the appointment of infinite Wisdom,—holding up the view that the Almighty had not only formed us after his own image, but he had given us the command over the beasts of the field, the fowls of the air, the fishes of the sea, and over every living thing that moveth upon the earth. And therefore, we have need of a divine wisdom to qualify us to act our part consistent with the important duties of our station; because, if we were governed and regulated as we ought to be, the creation at large would be happy. After this meeting I returned to my lodgings with a grateful heart. Next day, as no way opened for further public service, the time was spent in quiet contentment; being satisfied that he that believeth maketh not haste.

17th.—In the meeting at Chester, I felt concerned for the rising generation, and had occasion to deliver a short testimony,—pointing out the necessity of gaining a state of complete self-government, as well over the thoughts as over the actions;—remarking that unless our thoughts were rightly regulated, we should not be able rightly to worship our Creator, as we were in duty bound to do. To gain a perfect command, is a work of serious and great magnitude, and those who engage in it will find that there is an admirable fitness in the charge given by the blessed Saviour, to "watch and pray, lest we enter into temptation."

In the afternoon I was at an appointed meeting at Providence. It was a large gathering; and way opened to speak of the universality of the Christian religion,—and to show that the corner stone of this heavenly structure, is the manifestation of the spirit of God in the souls of men. In order to illustrate this doctrine, I mentioned the case of the conversion of Paul. This great minister to the Gentiles, when he submitted to the visitation of the spirit of God, was led minutely to consider his own condition,—and hence his mind took a view of the composition of man. In this view, he saw that we are beings composed of body, of spirit, and of soul. In his own case, he was satisfied that the soul was in bondage under the influence and power of the animal spirit; and hence it could not hold a connection with the Divine Spirit,—and was consequently subject to a spiritual death. To be redeemed from this bondage, was now the great point necessary to be gained. In considering how this was to be effected, he saw that nothing short of a divine gift could set him free from the law of sin and death; and it was his high consolation to find that this supernatural aid was given to him,—and he calls this unspeakable gift of God (the same by which the world was made) "the Word of God." And "this," he has said "is the Word of faith that we preach." "It is quick and powerful, sharp and sharper than any two-edged sword;" and it divides in man, as he submits himself to its operation, between the precious and the vile: and thus the soul comes to possess the power to rule and govern the animal nature in man; by which means a perfect state is gained, and "the law of the spirit of life in Christ Jesus, makes free from the law of sin and death."

Next day I was at a meeting at Springfield, where it seemed to me as if the true solemnity of feeling could not be gained: and I believed it was owing to a want of religious concern on the part of many present. The meeting, however, ended to my satisfaction. The day following, I was at a meeting at Haverford. It was smaller than I had expected; and I felt for awhile as though I should not be so clear of the neighborhood as I could wish; but when the meeting closed, my mind was free from any further engagement in that place. In the afternoon we rode to Merion, and lodged at the house of some young Friends of the name of Bowman.

20th.—I went to Manayunk, and made some attempt to have a meeting with the inhabitants. For a time it seemed doubtful whether an opportunity could be had with the people. It appeared that much had been done to prejudice their minds against us. We were accused of being disciples of Thomas Paine, and of course, infidels. It was said one of their ministers had made this charge. It seemed therefore the more necessary to make an effort to see the people together. At length a place was obtained for holding a meeting, which came together in the evening, and was a time of great favor; and it seemed to me as I was spreading before them what had opened upon my mind, that all their prejudices were removed, and I left them satisfied for the present.

21st.—This morning we parted with our kind friends, John Thomas and wife, and paid a short visit at Paul Jones's. After which we dined with an English Friend, George Greaves, and at four o'clock had an interesting meeting at Merion Square. The next day we had a meeting at a place called The Gulf: but few persons attended, and I found afterwards that some were prejudiced against meeting in the house.

Rested on the 23d, and the day following being first day, we were at Merion meeting. It was large, and proved to be an opportunity of great solemnity. I had some fears lest it might be injured by unnecessary additional communications,—but upon the whole I felt satisfied. In the afternoon we were present at a large and interesting meeting at Radnor. In this meeting I was led to mention the testimony of the apostle Paul, that "the natural man receiveth not the things of the spirit of God, but they are foolishness to him,—neither can he know them, because they are spiritually discerned." To illustrate the meaning of this text, I took notice of the natural man, and pointed out that his knowledge was obtained through the means of his corporeal senses, and however accurate he might be in the occupancy or use of those senses, as they were not adapted to the knowledge of spiritual objects,—so they could never embrace those of a spiritual character.

I was satisfied in the conclusion that this meeting had been a blessed opportunity. In the after part of the day we went to the house of Isaac Leedom and lodged there.

In a retrospect of my past life, many have been the trials and exercises through which I have passed; and it is cause of deep felt gratitude now in the evening of my day, to find nothing in my way,—and that my mind enjoys an unbroken confidence in the tender mercy of my God. Oh! how sweet are the incomes of his peace! and how powerful is the gathering arm of his love! I have known this in an eminent degree in the assemblies of the people; and not only so, but I have witnessed the truth of the apostle's testimony, that "there is no condemnation to them that are in Christ Jesus, who walk not after the flesh, but after the spirit." But great watchfulness and care are necessary, in order that we may at all times keep the cravings of our animal nature in subjection.

In the early part of the 10th month, I went to Philadelphia, and put up with my friend William Lindsay. On thinking of what my duty was in the city, the first clear opening was to appoint a meeting for the inhabitants of Kensington. But on some Friends going to get a place suitable for a meeting to be held in, no room could be had for that purpose. The concern remaining with me, at length on further search a large school room was obtained, and on first day evening, the 8th of the 10th month, I met a large company at that place. They were very solemn during the time I was engaged in speaking among them, and for some time after I sat down. The opportunity was quite satisfactory, and closed much to the relief of my mind. After the meeting had ended, several of the people assembled desired that they might have another meeting, and said that if I would admit of it, they had no doubt the meeting house would be filled full of people. I told them that for the present I was released, but if a concern should return, I would make another appointment, so I left them.

9th of the month and second of the week, I paid a number of visits among my friends, and in the evening went out of town, and was agreeably entertained at the house of my friend Joshua Longstreth. He had lately retuned from England, and as I also had been in that country, it was interesting to us to spend some time in conversing about Friends there. It was evident from his account that great changes have taken place since my visit among them, and that the society is on the decline in that land.

10th.—I returned to the city and spent the day making a number of social visits among my acquaintance. In the evening I was present at a meeting held in Spruce street meeting house. It was an opportunity that I hope will be long remembered to profit. Next day I attended Cherry street meeting; and was sorry to see so few of the members present. In the evening I had a large and solemn meeting at Green street. Here I was led to open the nature and effects of the ministry of the apostles, and to show that they did not speak of things that they knew not, but of those things that they saw, and felt, and heard. They were therefore not of the number that spake of other men's experiences so much as they did of their own.

I then rode to the house of my kind friend Joseph Briggs at Newtown, in Bucks county, and was at their meeting on first day: which was a comfortable opportunity. After which, in company with Joseph Briggs I paid a visit to my friends in New York, and was present at several of their meetings much to the comfort of my own mind, and to the satisfaction of those present. But the most memorable opportunity was on first day evening the 22d of 10th month. In this meeting my mind was livingly opened and I was engaged to call the attention of the assembly to the great concern of the redemption of the immortal soul. I was also led to take a view of many of the evils that were common in that large city—and to show the people that their theatres and various other places of amusement, were an offence in the divine sight.

After attending the meeting at Rose street, I felt that I was at liberty to leave the city, and return with my friend Joseph Briggs to his house. From thence I proceeded on my way to Baltimore, where I arrived on sixth day, the 27th of 10th month; and was comfortably accommodated at the house of my kinsman John Marsh. This Friend has for many years resided in Baltimore. He and his kind family are amply furnished with the means and the disposition to make their guests comfortable and happy. On seventh day I had the satisfaction of meeting with many of my old friends who came to attend their Yearly Meeting. It was cause of gratitude to be present with so many honest minds, and to witness their condescending conduct in attending to the duties of society. It was clear to me that they had a good Yearly Meeting, and were prepared to return home thankful that they had been together. During my stay in Baltimore, I was present at several public meetings for worship, which were also attended by a number of the citizens of the place, and they were favored opportunities. On the 4th of 11th month I left Baltimore and returned home.

I am convinced that the apostles and early professors of Christianity embraced the only powerful principle upon which not only the promulgation but the life of the Christian religion depends; that principle was and is the measure of the Spirit of God which is given to every man to profit withal. By this, that great minister to the Gentiles, to wit, Paul, was governed in all his labors in the gospel of Christ; and by this he knew that the gospel was the power of God unto salvation to all them that believe. But this power to which he earnestly recommended his brethren, he was afraid would be deserted by professors, even in his time; and he therefore admonished them to "Walk in the Spirit." Also when speaking of his own labors among them, he says, "And my speech and my preaching was not with enticing words of man's wisdom, but in demonstration of the spirit and of power; that your faith should not stand in the wisdom of men, but in the power of God." He had understood that some of them were saying, "I am of Paul; and I of Apollos; and I of Cephas." He saw that such were going from the Divine life, and regarding the outward polish and glitter of testimonies, rather than the pure power of the gospel; and therefore he was afraid of such lest he had bestowed upon them labor in vain.

Hence it is evident that a departure from the life and power of christianity, was early manifested. By degrees this party spirit spread, and more and more led away the professors, until they lost all confidence in the Truth of the doctrine of a divine gift to man, and denied the truth of divine revelation. Thus, they represented the Great Jehovah as a changeable being,—granting to one age the light of his spirit, and withholding it from another. And having concluded that revelation had ceased, and no further light was to be expected, they soon thought themselves wise enough not to need it.

It was out of this state of the professing church, that all the superstition and folly took place, which continued during the dark ages of the apostacy. Such were the effects of leaving the first principles embraced in the Christian church, and following those notions that were suited to the pride and folly of the natural man. Thus, it appears that the decline of Christianity and the reign of a dark night of apostacy, were the fruits of a departure from the light of Christ; for, had the professors of the Christian religion kept subject to this divine gift, the church never could have gone so entirely into a state of darkness and error as it did.

Therefore I have felt concerned to warn the society of Friends against entering upon this descending ground, and downward course. Friends in England departed from our profession, when they joined with those of other religious denominations for the purpose of spreading the scriptures among the eastern nations. When I was in England. I saw the impropriety of members of our society associating with others in that work, and mentioned to them, that if they felt a religious concern for spreading the Bible, they might be the people that were qualified to perform that service. But that I could not believe it was right for them to join with others in that business; especially when it was well known that the people of England acted upon principles which those who should receive the book could not believe were consistent with its doctrines. In these associations, Friends were soon exposed to the danger of balking those precious testimonies, in maintaining which our predecessors suffered so deeply.

As a religious society, all the duties we are called to fulfill in advancing the work of righteousness in the earth are to be fulfilled as acts of obedience, on our part, to the light of the spirit of God. But many of our parents are apparently joining with those who are acting their part in what are called works of reform, under the guidance of the natural understanding; for, among the people at large, the necessity for any higher principle to govern or influence, than the natural faculties of man,—is not admitted. Therefore when Friends join with them and attend their meetings, they cease to maintain a state of humble dependence upon the gospel power, and expect to be sufficiently wise of themselves.

Thus, as there is a joining with that subtle spirit of specious reasoning, which is cursed above every beast of the field, they will fall away from the true and safe standing, and lose the precious heavenly qualification to know the voice of the true Shepherd from the voice of the stranger. But if Friends keep to the true Guide and inward Director, they cannot be permitted to join with any in promoting religious concern, who do not believe in the influence of the Divine Spirit as a necessary qualification for every good work.

I am aware that these will be considered as narrow-minded sentiments. But when we look at the profession which Friends have made, and see that while they abide in this profession and living principle, the

12

world must come to them ;—and that, if they leave this ground and go to others, it almost amounts to a certainty that the testimonies we are called to support, of the reality of the divine gift to man must fall. Hence we may see that there is great danger of the pure principle being deserted, by those who are connecting themselves with such as do not think of waiting for any better light than their own rational powers.

The 1st of the 4th month, 1839, I attended Buckingham Monthly Meeting. In it my mind was deeply affected on account of the existence of a disorganizing spirit among Friends, which if not checked will sooner or later divide the society. I took occasion to remark that I had never known a society that had embraced a higher profession than we did; nor was it possible for any to profess higher. But the business was, to live agreeable to the profession,—which I feared was not the case with too many. It is a sorrowful fact, that many who are brought up among Friends, seem to understand but little about the principles or testimonies of Truth.

During this week I attended a marriage, and the entertainment though sufficient, was the most moderate that I ever met with; for the drink was only water.

13th.—At meeting at Buckingham; and while I was quietly looking toward the end of life, my mind was brought under the humbling power of the gospel; and by its blessed influence I was led to deliver a testimony to the importance of following after those things which make for peace, and things wherewith one may edify another. It was a satisfactory meeting; and the afternoon was spent in writing a letter to my only child.

14th.—This morning my mind was turned to the great Fountain of all good, and I felt thankful for his providential care over me. I could see that though I was numbered among the poor of this world, yet I might say that having nothing I possessed all things necessary to my comfort and happiness. It appeared to me to be a great privilege to be free from all the causes of worldly care and anxiety now in the evening of life.

O my good and merciful Lord, thou knowest all things; thou knowest that I wish to fulfill every thing that is required of me; and there is no power nor wisdom that can guide me, but thine alone. Through a long life I have been supported and kept by thee, and therefore I have ample cause at all times to confide in thee, the alone helper of thy people.

16th.—Awaking this morning, after a night of irregular sleep, I found all within was peaceful and quiet. It was a satisfaction to find, that even while sleeping no evil principle had led the mind away from the adorable Fountain of life and salvation. I have known times when the mind, during sleep, has been drawn away, and submitted to do things that were not right. It grieved me much, and I have on awaking rejoiced to find it was only a dream. It seems to me, however, that the mind may grow up to such a happy state, as, sleeping or waking, always to resist evil.

17th.—Our meetings here are often seasons of trial. The living must feel the state of the meeting, nor can they expect often to rise above it. Sometimes it seems like having a table spread in the presence of enemies.

19th.—My prospect is in favor of returning to

Chester county; but as a poor pilgrim on earth, I know not where I may be accommodated, having no fixed residence, and no means by which to secure one.

O my gracious God, grant me patience and resignation to wait the appointed time until my change come. Thou knowest all my lonesome hours, and unavoidable gloomy feelings. Ah! my gracious God! thou art my only company; and when I can feel thy living presence, all is well. In going now to the great city, O Father of lights and of spirits, condescend to be with me, and keep my life pure by the word of thy grace,—that so I may neither say nor do any thing to grieve thy Holy Spirit. It was my joy and my comfort, when in the morning of my days I was turned from the follies of the world; and now in the evening of my time, I can look to the end in full confidence that I shall not be a cast-away. O holy Father, my soul can now praise thy excellent name, and rejoice in thy salvation. Glory and honor, and thanksgiving and praise belong to thee now and for ever; for thy promises are all fulfilled; and no one ever trusted in thee, and was confounded. Thou art the strength of thy people, and their exceeding great reward.

On the 31st of the 1st month, 1840, I left my present home in company with Joseph S. Walton, with the view of performing a visit in the love of the gospel to Friends in New Jersey. We proceeded on to Darby, and lodged at Rachel Hunt's. The evening was spent in pleasant and instructive conversation; and I could but admire the lively and happy disposition of this ancient Friend. Next day we rode to Woodbury, and were accommodated at the house of William Cooper. The day following we attended Woodbury meeting, which was large, and it appeared to be mercifully owned by the prevalence of a blessed solemnity. The doctrine preached seemed to meet the witness for Truth in the hearts of the people, and I felt a hope that it was not in vain. With great clearness of mind I was led to treat of the confidence of the apostle Paul in his own case, when he said he had fought the good fight, and that he had kept the faith, and had finished his course, and that henceforth there was laid up for him a crown of righteousness, which God the righteous Judge would give him; and not him only, but to all those who loved the appearance of our Lord Jesus Christ. In allusion to the conversion of this great minister, I was led to give an instructive view of the component nature of man,—and particularly to show that Paul considered the animal nature in man as the vessel of dishonor,—and that those who lived in the gratification of the appetites and passions of this nature, would fail to fight the good fight of faith, and consequently be unprepared for the Divine acceptance.

In opening those views, it was evident that the meeting was deeply interested. I saw that there was an energy and dignity in the gospel, that could not be equalled by any imitation of it.

Third of 2d month we were at Upper Greenwich meeting. It was not very large; but in spreading before them some views that I received of the nature of man, and the work of his redemption from under the dominion of his animal nature, I felt convinced that it had a happy and solemnizing effect. I remarked that the little leaven spoken of in the parable, was hid in three measures of meal; and why *three* was the number mentioned, had been a subject of some consideration. It however appeared to me to correspond with the apostle Paul's view of the component nature of man, which consists of three parts—body, spirit, and soul. It appears that the judgment of the apostle was, that the Divine Principle, which he calls the Word of God, was capable of completing the reformation of man. He saw that this Word was "quick and powerful,"—that it divided between soul and spirit;—giving to the more noble part—to the immortal soul—the power to govern the animal passions and appetites; and thus leavening the whole man into its own perfect character. Having explained the doctrine of man's redemption upon those principles, it was satisfactory to find a happy solemnity spread over the meeting. After meeting we rode to Abel Robins' and lodged there.

In journeying thus far, I find the duty to be solemn and weighty. When I enter the meeting-houses, and see such numbers of people assembled at my request, I am conscious that I have no treasures in store for them, and that I myself am a poor dependent being. This has a tendency to introduce the mind into a state of deep humility. But hitherto I have found the gracious promises of my God fulfilled—that he would be mouth and wisdom, tongue and utterance.

4th.—We were at Mullica Hill meeting. In this opportunity it was occasion of gratitude to be again favored with the needful qualification to advocate the cause of righteousness. The minds of Friends were directed to the *unspeakable gift of God.* This gift was spoken of as being the great regulating Principle that would, if followed, complete the work of man's redemption and salvation.

There are times when the poor servant feels as if he had nothing at his command. But when we are weak, we should not forget that even then the Shepherd of his flock is strong, and that he can command even the very stones of the street to break forth into singing. So that there is no necessity to look forward with any anxiety about the future, but wisely leave all to the government of the Holy Head; nothing doubting the sufficiency both of his wisdom and power to govern and direct all things according to his own blessed will.

6th.—Had a solemn meeting at Woodstown. In this opportunity my mind was livingly introduced into a view of the mercy of God, as manifested in the case of the poor man who fell among thieves. It appeared to me that in this passage we were furnished with an admirable proof of the goodness of God to his finite creature man. It was evident that this man was on his way to the city of corruption; but notwithstanding this was the case, Divine kindness followed him, and a way was made for his restoration.

In the course of my testimony, it was encouraging to witness the prevalence of a precious solemnity; and I felt my mind drawn forth in deep solicitude for the salvation of the inhabitants of this neighborhood. So another meeting was appointed for to-morrow. We lodged at Thomas Davis's, who has lately been affected with palsy on his left side. He appeared to be in a happy and gathered state of mind.

7th.—I was present at another large meeting at Pilesgrove, or Woodstown. In this opportunity I was led to show that Friends have been wrongfully charged with denying the divinity of Christ. I thought it was right for me to deny this charge, and to inform the assembly that we believe that all the wondrous works performed by the blessed Jesus were accomplished by the immediate power of God. And as this was the fact, we were prepared to unite with the apostle Paul in the confession, that "to us there is but one God, by whom and for whom are all things." When an individual submits to be regulated and governed by the gift of the Spirit of God, there is a change perfected in his case, and he becomes another kind of being: and from living in the ferocity of his animal passions, he now embraces the lamb-like nature. And that state being gained, it stands as the atonement for all the sins that are past.

On the 8th we rode to Salem and lodged at Joseph Bassetts. Next day attended Salem meeting, and it was a favored opportunity. The doctrine delivered was in the demonstration of the Spirit and with power; and it was evident that the minds of many present were baptized by the clear light of the testimony of Truth. The day following we had a satisfactory meeting at Alloways Creek.

11th.—This evening I had a large meeting at Salem, in which my mind was livingly opened in a view of the spirituality of the doctrines of the Christian religion. The subjects on which I was led to speak were introduced by mentioning the testimony of the apostle Paul, that "the natural man receiveth not the things of the Spirit of God; for they are foolishness unto him; neither can he know them, because they are spiritually discerned." In treating of this testimony, I was led to show that the means of knowledge to the natural man were confined to his corporeal senses, and that these could only embrace things natural. Therefore, until we experience the spiritual senses brought into action, we must remain ignorant of things spiritual. It was evident that the communication produced a deep and solemn effect, and the meeting ended to satisfaction.

12th.—I rode back to Woodstown, and attended the Quarterly meeting of ministers and elders. It was a comfort to find in this meeting a number of valuable members who love the Truth, and with whom I felt a portion of the unity of the Spirit in the bond of peace. Next day I was at the Quarterly meeting for discipline; and I think I have seldom, if ever, witnessed the stream of the gospel to rise higher in any meeting, than it did in this.

The 14th we rode to Woodbury, and had a large evening meeting. In this opportunity I was favored to preach the gospel of the Son of God with much clearness; showing that the divinity of the Son was that same wisdom and power that was manifested by Jesus of Nazareth in all his wonderful works, and the miracles which he performed in the land of Judea; and that, by submitting to the death of the cross, he confirmed by his example the glorious doctrines that he had publicly preached to the people. The meeting closed much to my comfort.

16th.—I attended Moorestown meeting, and next day had a meeting at Westfield. Although the life was not felt to be in dominion at these meetings as at most of the others I have attended, yet I felt glad that I had been with them, and had received instruction. After the latter meeting, we dined at William Evans'. This Friend is eighty years of age, and has a vigorous constitution.

In journeying along thus far, I have been favored with good health, and in all the meetings I have attended, it has been cause of thankful admiration to be enabled to clear my mind of every impression of duty; and I cannot doubt that so far as I have gone, it has been in conformity with the openings of Truth.

On the 18th we attended Evesham meeting. It was large, and a comfortable opportunity. Although I had a close and searching testimony to deliver among them, yet I felt convinced that the great Head of the church was with us, affording light and understanding rightly to divide the word preached in that assembly. In the conclusion I felt the inward evidence of Divine approbation. There is no outward circumstance that I meet with, that affords greater cause for gratitude, than that of being safely led through a testimony in a large assembly. It has been my privilege in the course of this journey to feel the sustaining power of Truth in every service to which I have been called.

19.—This evening we had a large and solemn meeting at Moorestown. I have seldom felt better satisfied with any religious opportunity. There was a remarkable stillness prevailed throughout the whole time of the meeting. At the conclusion I recommended the people to read the sixth chapter of Matthew.

We next had a solid opportunity with Friends and others at Rancocas; and the next day had a meeting at Upper Evesham, in which I was favored to deliver an instructive testimony. Here I was persuaded that some people were injured by a zeal for God, that was not according to knowledge; and being ignorant of the righteousness which is of faith, they were going about to establish their own righteousness. Hence, they were much employed with their prayer meetings; and in these opportunities they were full of words, and could approach the Divine Being as if he were a man like themselves. I told them if they would read the sixth chapter of Matthew, they would find much useful instruction on the subject. We lodged at Caleb Shreve's, and next day went on to Mount Holly.

On first day morning, the 23d of 2d month, we attended a large meeting at Mount Holly, with which I was satisfied. Next day the Quarterly meeting of ministers and elders was held, and I thought them a valuable company of Friends. On the day following, I was at the Quarterly meeting for discipline, held at Mount Holly. I next had a satisfactory meeting at Bordentown, and lodged at Aaron Ballangee's.

28th.—Had a meeting at Crosswicks. During the communication offered in this assembly, I felt that the power of the gospel was indeed above every power; and it appeared to me that if all who profess to be ministers of the gospel of Christ kept to the plain and simple openings of it, the credit of the ministry would stand much higher than it does at present. There is cause to lament over a ministry that is not in the life of Truth; yet there are some precious plants coming forward, who will be ornaments in their day, if they keep to the Divine gift, and are not led away by the will of man.

28th.—We were at an interesting meeting at Trenton, and next day had a meeting at Mansfield, in which my mind was opened into a general view of the true church, that was gathered by the Word of God out of all nations, kindreds, tongues, and people. By the same Divine principle, all the children of God, of every generation were saved. It was the word nigh in the heart, and in the mouth, and was the Word of faith which was preached by the apostles, and true believers in the primitive church. A precious silence prevailed throughout, under which the meeting closed.

3d month 3d.—We were at Haddonfield meeting, which was large, and I was of the mind that some profitable impressions were made. Next day we attended Camden meeting, and it proved to be a time of instruction and encouragement to Friends. I then felt at liberty to return home. After lodging at Joseph Kaighn's, we crossed the river, and arrived at home next day, the 6th of the month. I felt a satisfaction in a retrospect of the journey, being persuaded that it was a happy devotion of our time to the great work of universal righteousness. In all places that we visited, we were kindly entertained by our friends, and had cause to acknowledge the goodness of our holy Helper in furnishing a clear evidence of the services into which I was called. There is an enjoyment in the performance of our duty that is better felt than it can be described.

3d month 13th, 1840.—I have returned from performing a religious visit to a number of meetings in New Jersey. During my travels, it was pleasant to find many valuable members of the Society; and among them there are a number of young persons who appear to be making a right beginning. But they are exposed to many dangers, and can only be preserved by keeping faithful to the great Shepherd of the sheep.

I have seen that there is a disposition to be doing something by taking an active part with those who are not of us; and who, instead of waiting for the Divine

Guide to put them forth, are always ready: and as these run unsent, they cannot prosper the work. It is now, as it always has been, that the great Author of all good "will not give his glory to another, nor his praise to graven images." All therefore who are useful in his work, must be guided by his wisdom in all their movements. Such will wait upon the Divine gift, and never attempt any thing of themselves.

It has also appeared to me that if the members of our Society join with other people, and carry their concerns out of the Society, they will in this way weaken themselves; and by carrying their concerns abroad, they will weaken the travail of the church. Whereas, if they would keep to their individual exercises, until they had ripened in their own minds, they would then be opened in the church with weight, and be acted upon according to the mind of Truth; and as no good effort rightly made is ever lost, a happy effect would be produced. The members being thus united, and moving together, would be a strength to one another; and the unity of the Spirit, which is the bond of peace, would be preserved.

In our reflections upon the degraded and suffering condition of the oppressed African race, it is not marvellous that our sympathy should be powerfully excited, and that we should feel anxious to do something for their relief. But we may remember with instruction, that Divine Goodness knows and sees all their afflictions, and in his own time he will open a way for their complete relief.

It is quite probable that Pharaoh and his people thought they held the Israelites by a tie that could not be broken. But while they were supposing they had them perfectly secure, the Almighty had determined that they should be released. He therefore appeared to Moses, on the back side of the desert in the burning bush, and said to him "I have seen, I have seen the affliction of my people which is in Egypt, and I have heard their groaning, and am come down to deliver them." He then informed Moses that he was to be his messenger to Pharaoh to demand their freedom. We may remark the reluctance of Moses to go on this important errand to the king of Egypt: but after Divine Mercy had showed him his power, and put him in possession of means by which to convince those to whom he was sent, that the Great Jehovah had sent him, he went to his brethren, and to Pharaoh on the solemn errand, and told Pharaoh to let the people go that they might serve him. The great business was now begun. Pharaoh was apprised that he must let these people go. Nor was there any abatement of the demand, until the people of Egypt determined to drive them out.

Thus we may see that Divine Goodness in his own way and time took up the cause of his afflicted people, and completed their deliverance. By this wonderful interposition of Almighty power and goodness, we may see in the first place, that the Great Father of mankind not only sees but compassionates the sufferings of his creatures, and in his own time will deliver them, and lead them to a land of promise. In the second place we may observe that they had been in bondage four hundred and thirty years; and not until the expiration of that period was there a Moses raised up to plead their cause. It was then that the fire appeared on the back side of the desert in a burning bush, and the bush was not consumed It was then a Moses was brought to see this great sight, that the bush burned and was not consumed. And here he was not only informed that a gracious God had seen the affliction of his people, but that he had come down to relieve them from all their oppressions.

Here we may see that He who inhabits eternity, and whose name is Holy, not only regards the situation of his creatures, but in his own time makes a way for their enlargement. It was so with the children of Israel; and it must be so with the people of the African race. But if we take a deliberate view of the African race, and consider their situation, and of their being brought to America, it appears to be one of those cases that we may believe is under the notice of a superintending Providence; and I cannot doubt that in his own time and way he will complete their deliverance from the state of bondage and degradation that they are in. I cannot therefore but wish, that as Friends are the only people who acknowledge the Divine Spirit as the only safe and sure Guide to man,—they would, in this concern, carefully mind the light of Truth in themselves, and keep out of all the mixtures that are in the world in relation to the subject of the emancipation of the enslaved African race.

Although I have no idea that the society of Friends should think of other classes of professing Christians as being inferior to themselves;—yet, as we believe we have been separated from them by the spirituality of our profession, it appears to me that the only way for us to fulfill the duty we owe to the great cause of universal righteousness is to act our part alone. We are not prepared to move or act with others, because we profess to be governed and actuated by the impulses of a higher principle than they do ; for other professors do not pretend to believe in or wait for any divine influence communicated to man, as we do. Therefore, if we act up to the truth of our doctrine, we cannot do it consistently in connection with others who do not see the necessity of waiting for such influence. But by our remaining together and faithfully following the impressions of the Divine Guide, as they are clearly opened to us, we shall be more likely to perform our duties correctly.

When Friends were separated from the rest of mankind, we know they were a persecuted people ; and to this day they stand very much alone in a doctrinal point of view. Until other professors become willing to admit the truth of their profession, I can see no propriety in Friends joining with them in carrying out the testimonies of Truth. It is a fact that the doctrine we hold of waiting for the manifestation and qualifying influence of the Spirit, is a persecuted doctrine by many. And as the testimonies of Truth held by Friends, can only be promoted in the world by the power of the Principle from whence they proceed, it can, in my view, be the only safe way for the society to keep together, and carefully fulfill what they find to do in the clear manifestations of the Light of Christ.

4th mo. 2d.—Time is passing on, and so far as I can see, I am now quietly in my place. No doubt every period of life has its duties ; and I esteem it a privilege when I can have a clear sight of mine. When we are wholly given up to do the Lord's will, it is not often that we are at a loss in understanding it. Our greatest difficulty in gaining a correct judgment, is chargeable to ourselves. The light of Truth is always present with the honest and upright mind; but many live in great degrees of uncertainty, from not having their own wills brought into subjection to the divine will. There is no condition more desirable than that of the perfectly passive state. It is when this is our attainment, that we are free from all anxiety. Many are kept in anxiety and trouble by anticipation. They picture to themselves difficulties which never take place; and thus disturb their own feelings and sometimes the comfort of others. If we properly considered the laws of Infinite Wisdom, we should probably find that our situation in this world was rendered as favorable as we could reasonably desire, and that the wants of nature are few and easily supplied. It is from indulging in wrong habits that we are landed in difficulty. The doctrine of the primitive believers was, that "we brought nothing into this world, and it is certain that we can take nothing with us out of it." Therefore, according to their belief, "having food and raiment, we should therewith be content." Those who are not so, do but make trials and difficulties for themselves.

4th mo. 11th, 1840.—I was at a Monthly Meeting, in which I felt my mind tried with a circumstance that occurred; and which I considered to be out of the order of Friends. There was an appearance in prayer, and during the time of vocal supplication, several persons kept their seats, and did not rise nor uncover the head. Considering this practice, I felt tried; because I could not believe that such conduct would ever be the means of building one another up in that faith that overcometh the world. In my reflections upon the subject, my views were extended to the principles upon which religious society should be formed. There is no principle of equal value to the existence of religious society with that of unity. If once the unity of society is lost, all that will be left will be of little value. Hence, I conclude that any part of the conduct of a Friend which strikes at the unity of the body is dangerous, and should be carefully guarded against.

4th mo. 19th.—Since the death of my esteemed friend Mary Lukens, it has seemed proper for me to spend some time with the family she has left. Her husband, Daniel Lukens, is much afflicted with a local disease; and in reflecting upon his case, my sympathy has been much excited. I find it is a valuable attainment to be resigned to our situation, and patiently to wait the Lord's time for our release: for his time we must believe is the best time. When we are the subjects of pain and disease, there is sometimes a tendency in our nature to covet that a change might come; and hence we are liable to the danger of becoming impatient. But if we indulge in that state of feeling, we only increase our own suffering. The mind that can retain a steady condition, is always the most happy in the end.

In my reflections upon the variety which we have to pass through in the journey of life, it has appeared to me that kind Providence has subjected us to no one circumstance, but with a design that each of them should be useful, and tend to promote our improvement. King David said of himself, "Before I was afflicted I went astray." This may be the common tendency of the human race, but it does not appear to me to be necessarily so. I view it rather as a consequence of the want of watchfulness and true devotion of mind.

4th mo. 20th.—I was at the Western Quarterly Meeting of Ministers and Elders. In this meeting Friends were much tried with a zealous woman who seemed to think that much was laid upon her in consequence of the decline of Friends from a faithful regard to their religious principles. But I saw that her zeal was not governed by a proper knowledge of the real state of things ; and therefore her communications only went to interrupt the minds of others, and hinder them from being gathered to the proper state of feeling, and of learning our true condition.

During the consideration of the Queries, a dear old father delivered a living and reaching testimony, which had the effect to stir up the pure mind, and edify the meeting. I rejoiced that he was so favored, and added my testimony to the justice of his concern,—fully believing that he had presented a view that should seriously engage the attention of all present.

Next day the Quarterly Meeting for business came together, in which I was led back to the Mosaic account of creation,—and that when the earth was without form and void, and darkness was upon the face of the deep, God said Let there be light; and there was light. It appeared to me that this great principle, both in the material and the spiritual world, could only come from him who is declared to be "Light, and in him is no darkness at all." In pursuing the opening before me, I was led to show that the apostle Paul, by the manifestations of this light, found that he was a persecutor. And hence he was led into a deep and serious inquiry into his own nature, and the causes why he had been landed on such erroneous ground. By this important search into himself, he became acquainted with the composition of man, and therefore gave his testimony that "that was not first which is spiritual,—but that which is natural." In which he fully agreed with the account given of the creation of man,—that his body and the animal spirit were first formed, and afterward the Creator breathed into his nostrils the breath of life, by which man became a living soul. Here, we have evidence of the state of union between the Creator and the creature. Now to preserve this union is the great design and object of true religion ; and this is only known and witnessed by those who experience the animal nature subjected in them to the divine. The testimony was owned by a deep and solemn feeling in the meeting.

2d of 8th month, 1840.—I am now in the close of my seventy-second year. My thoughts continue to be active in the various concerns of the day. After the experience of a middling long life, I see no cause to doubt the truth of the principle professed by Friends, and their belief in the manifestation of the Divine gift of God to man. And it seems to me that if they are faithful in following this heavenly Guide, they must continue to be a light to the world, and advance the cause of universal righteousness. Already it is evident that they have been instrumental in holding up many valuable testimonies. The rights of conscience have been plead by them; and mankind now agree to a large extent that it is a principle which no human authority can control, or has any right to interfere with in matters relating to our duty toward the Supreme Being.

Other testimonies are also embraced in the profession of Friends, that are of great value to mankind. Witness their doctrine in relation to oaths,—a hireling ministry, and bearing of arms. Each of these is a testimony so important to the human family, that they should all be kept in view and faithfully maintained with the greatest integrity and care. On the subject of the ministry, their testimony to its purity and freedom is of sufficient importance to demand the most rigid attention. If the Society should ever let fall this testimony, it will be a departure from a great Christian obligation, and an immense loss to the subject of the spreading of the light of the glorious gospel.

Besides the preceding valuable points of the principles of Truth, Friends have adopted the most rational and perfect mode of social worship, that is to be met with; because they meet and sit in silence. In this state every mind has the opportunity of attending to its own condition; and if it holds to a state of union with the divine gift, it may in the silent state of the meeting, be prepared devoutly to worship God in spirit and in truth. Again, if an individual in the meeting should be sensible of having been unfaithful, or disobedient, and therefore should feel condemnation,—there is the advantage of silently attending to its own case; and thus the mind may become prepared (by a deep-felt spiritual repentance) to return with honest integrity to its merciful Creator, and renew its covenant with him: in which case it has gained a qualification to worship in the beauty of holiness.

Not only have these silent opportunities an advantage in favor of honest integrity, but they put it in the power of the sincere-hearted to feel after, and to understand their real condition, their spiritual state. But when an assembly are met together for the purpose of divine worship and religious improvement,—and immediately on entering their meeting-house, begin to pray, or sing, or in any other manner become active,—there is great reason to doubt the soundness of their proceedings ; because it is quite probable that the services they so hastily engage in have no higher principle than the mere will and activity of the creature. And though such may seem to kindle a fire, or warmth of zeal, and to move in the light of the sparks thereof,—they may find the effects of this creaturely activity to be as declared by the prophet, " This shall ye have of mine hand, ye shall lie down in sorrow."

8th mo. 9th, 1840.—Being now a member of Fallowfield Monthly Meeting, I was favored in one of our religious opportunities with some views of the attribute of mercy that were instructive ; and it appeared to me to be my duty to make the following remarks on the subject. We may hold a belief in the existence of this wonderful attribute, and yet not be proper objects for it to act upon. Those who witness the precious enjoyment of this divine attribute, are such as sincerely abhor all evil, and are endeavoring to be conformed to the heavenly Father's will. Such are coming out of the follies of the world, and are entering into the divine life, and to these is the attribute of mercy extended. But while people are living in the indulgence of the passions and propensities of the natural mind, they stand in a state of wilful disobedience, and therefore are not children of the kingdom and government of Christ. For, in order to become members of his church, it is necessary that he alone should rule and govern all our actions. Such as these are the objects of his mercy, and it is his good pleasure to own them by his blessed light, truth, and spirit, in their hearts. To such is the heavenly Father's love, and his mercy is over them for good, while they continue to walk in his law.

12th.—This evening I was led into a state of serious thoughtfulness on the solemnity of the Divine admonitions. I think I have never known a season of so much heavy thunder, nor heard of so much destruction of property by the lightning. I cannot believe that all these awful thunderings are the mere consequence of the common course of the elements. Doubtless, Divine Providence has certain fixed laws and principles that usually operate in the general course of all nature. But when a large number of buildings and property is destroyed in one day, and in a particular neighborhood, it seems right that it should lead the mind into some serious inquiries, whether there is not a special cause for the dispensation of those awful events.

On the 14th, in company with Joseph S. Walton and wife, I attended the funeral of Samuel Pennock. As my mind was preserved in a state of inward attention to the impressions of the divine gift, I found a concern to invite the company into the meeting-house, and a blessed meeting we had. He that promised to be to his people a present help in every needful time, graciously condescended to favor us with light and understanding, and by his heavenly aid the gospel was preached in the life and simplicity of its own character; and it appeared that many minds were visited with the renewal of the glorious day-spring from on high. I returned to my present peaceful home with a mind at rest and peace in itself.

On the 15th of the 10th month, 1840, William Ellis, from Monallen, and Caleb Ogborn, from New Market, were at our meeting. William's testimony was lively and feeling. I felt much sympathy with him, as a plain honest man, and wished him encouraged to a faithful discharge of his duty; he being one of those humble-minded men that have come into the society by convincement.

24th.—I attended our meeting at Fallowfield, and had an important testimony to deliver on the great advantages of waiting on the Lord. The meeting was solemnized, and ended in the life.

11th mo. 7th.—I attended our Monthly Meeting, of Fallowfield, held at Doe Run meeting-house. On my arrival there I was agreeably surprised by seeing two of my old acquaintances and friends, James Walton and Joseph Briggs. I found they had left their homes and rode upwards of forty miles on purpose to see me, and know how I was situated, and what state they could report my mind to be in. It appeared that some who had gone from Friends had reported that I had become melancholy, and was rendered useless. It is marvellous how men can delight in detraction and in spreading false reports. But when they become deluded, they can make even lies their refuge: every work, however, has its appropriate reward, whether it be good, or whether it be evil.

Having opened in our Monthly Meeting a concern to visit Warrington Quarterly Meeting, and some meetings on the way, it was united with, and a Minute furnished me for the occasion. I accordingly set out on the 18th of the 11th month, 1840, having Joseph S. Walton for my companion. We stopped a short time in Columbia, where, amidst the rejoicings of the people on account of the election of President, one man had his arm broken by the unlooked-for discharge of a cannon, and others were in great danger of losing their lives.

On seventh day, the 21st, the meeting of ministers and elders met. They were a small company; but in sitting quietly among them, I felt thankful in being impressed with a clear sense that they were mercifully cared for by the Head of the church. And a hope was entertained that if they continue faithful, there will be a gathering and increase of Society. Next day the public meeting was mercifully crowned with a deep felt solemnity. I have seldom witnessed the power of Truth to be in such admirable dominion as in this meeting. I was led to show that the work of man's salvation consisted in a perfect conquest over the natural spirit; and also that this was a change which christianity called for; likewise, that the apostle Paul in all his ministry pointed to this victory as a state of the triumph of the soul of man over the animal nature.

On the 23d, the Quarterly Meeting assembled, and it appeared to be a solemn and important meeting. In it I was led to open views of the necessity of obedience to the gift of God, as the only means of being saved from all iniquity. The meeting ended with much satisfaction, and in the evening following we had a precious opportunity where we lodged.

On fourth day, the 25th, we were at Huntington meeting. It was an opportunity in which I was led to urge upon the assembly the awful necessity there was rightly to improve the time, in order that they might be fitted and prepared to enter the eternal world. In this meeting my mind was much humbled under a sense of the mercy and grace furnished to that assembly. In the evening I had an important opportunity with a number of Friends, in which I succeeded in convincing most that were present, that as a Society, we were called to peace; that in order to obey this call it was necessary that we should remember that our holy Head had declared that his kingdom was not of this world; but that it stood in the peaceable, lamblike nature and spirit. Hence I inferred that the members of it should keep out of all strife and contention, and set an example of complete separation from all the noises and tumults that are going on among men; for I could not see how Friends were to maintain the peaceable testimony with consistency, and at the same time take a part in the political contests that were agitated in the world.

26th.—We parted with Friends at Huntington, and rode to Yorktown, where I had an appointed meeting with the inhabitants. It was a memorable opportunity, in which many minds were solemnized by the blessed power of the gospel of Christ, and I was glad to find much tenderness among the people. Visits were also made to sundry other places, much to my satisfaction. At Berlin, however, it was a time of trial, but ended under a satisfactory solemnity. To me it is always cause of thankfulness, when the people are brought into a state of true silence. It is then that I believe the voice of the Shepherd and Bishop of souls is heard, and the company benefited.

I was also at some places not much visited by

Friends, and it appeared to be particularly encouraging to many of the inhabitants to find that they had been thought of in this way.

After my return home, my thoughts were often engaged in a view of some of the transactions that are going on in the Society of Friends; and I have had my fears that all things are not as they should be. The part that is taken by some of our members, is of an active kind; and I am afraid it will be said to them by the great Judge of quick and dead, "Who hath required this at your hands?" If it be an activity that has its origin in the first or earthy nature, it will not be approved by Him who has declared that he will not give his glory to another, nor his praise to graven images.

On the 25th of the 5th month, 1841, accompanied by my kind friend, Joseph S. Walton, I left my present residence, with a view of paying a religious visit eastward, as far as Nantucket. We called at Westchester, and spent a little time with my daughter, who has been much confined with sickness in her family through the past winter. Thence we went on to Philadelphia, and took the cars for New York, where we arrived on the 26th, and were kindly received at Dobel Baker's. Here I had a visit from Rachel Barker and her husband.

28th.—I attended two sittings of the Yearly Meeting, in both which it appeared to me that Friends understood one another, and they were satisfactory seasons. In making my observations on Friends of this Yearly Meeting, it was comfortable to find that brotherly love and kind feelings prevailed among them. In one of the sittings of this Yearly Meeting, I made some remarks on the value of Friends living in subjection and obedience to the Divine gift; showing that it was only as this was the case and practice of Friends, that the life and power of God reigned over all. After the business of the meeting was concluded, a solemn pause took place, and Friends separated under a grateful sense that they had been favored together in transacting the concerns that came before them.

After this I went on board the steamboat called the "Narragansett," and by reason of a thick fog we were kept on board till twelve o'clock on seventh day. Then went on and arrived at New Bedford in the night. On first day I was at two satisfactory meetings there.

We lodged at the house of William Rotch, who lives here in the full enjoyment of ample means, and the disposition to accommodate his friends, and make them comfortable. In this town, which is handsomely situated on the sea shore, there are many houses that appear like palaces; one of which was pointed out to me, that cost in building, eighty thousand dollars! Such are certainly not proper examples for Friends; yet in this place there is much that goes to prove that the wealth of the world has very much led away some from the principles of moderation, plainness, and simplicity, as professed by the Society.

On the afternoon of second day, I made some visits to the aged and afflicted. One was to Ann Rotch, the daughter of my old friend, James Smith, of Philadelphia. She was in poor health, and aware of her situation. I was pleased to find her possessed of so much clearness of judgment, and correctness of views, and it seemed to me that she might come to a happy close.

Another visit I made to the widow of Samuel Rodman. Here we had a religious opportunity, which seemed to be a favored one. This dear friend was then turned of eighty years old, and still vigorous and lively. In these visits I had the company of Sarah Underwood, a valuable minister from the Genessee country. Next day we embarked on board a steamboat, and had an agreeable passage to Nantucket, where we arrived about five o'clock, and went to the house of Nathaniel Barney.

6th month, 2d.—After taking a ride to the margin of the ocean, and viewing the awful grandeur of the returning waves, beating in endless succession upon the sandy beach, we returned to the town, and at half-past seven o'clock proceeded to an appointed meeting. It was a time of trial, from a sense of great indifference to the concerns of true religion. But feeling my mind acted upon by a necessity to advocate the great cause, I rose and communicated what seemed to be given me; and found by continuing in the patient travail, that life was in some degree felt, and the meeting concluded under a sense that the cause of Truth had not suffered by it. Next day I attended Friends' week-day meeting, in which I felt my way to remind them of the great obligations we are under to the Giver of every good and perfect gift, for the merciful influences of his blessed Spirit, by which we are put in mind of our duty, and by which also we may see how to stand in the divine sight.

4th.—I looked round the town of Nantucket, and found it to be a place of but little regularity. There are great establishments for preparing the oil for use which is obtained by whaling; and there are large quantities of spermaceti candles made here. Those who are engaged in this kind of business must employ a large capital. There is danger in such large concerns of worldly business, of the mind becoming too much engrossed therein, and thereby being led away from that state of watchfulness and careful attention to duties of a more exalted nature, becoming beings formed for the enjoyment of immortality and eternal life.

We visited several persons advanced in life, one of whom was a man turned of ninety years of age, who had lost his eye-sight. This man makes no complaint about any thing. He thinks the time of his stay here a subject with which he has nothing to do; but that it is his duty to wait patiently until his change comes. It was instructive to me to be convinced by the example of this individual, that it is possible to be so disciplined as to be perfectly at rest on the margin of eternity.

6th.—I am convinced that Friends here have much in their power, if they would but keep subject to the blessed government of Christ, our holy Head. In that case an example would be set that would have a very convincing effect upon others. We attended their two meetings held this day; and although I did not find the life and power of Truth to rise into dominion in so eminent a manner as has sometimes been the case, yet the opportunities were favored with a good degree of solemnity, and I parted with Friends under a feeling of gospel affection.

This evening, in a parting opportunity with a number of Friends, a solid and deep feeling was experienced, under which a door was opened to pray to God for the glorious coming and advancement of his own righteous cause of Truth in the earth. The minds of those present were rendered near and dear to one another, in the pure feeling of the blessed gospel of Christ, the Saviour of men.

In passing about among Friends on this island, I perceived they were in the habit of much conversation. I felt the want of stillness, and was desirous to promote a disposition of retirement; believing that as Friends get off from this inward, attentive state, they suffer a serious loss, and become weakened, so as to depart from that lively feeling in which a knowledge of the mind of Truth is gained.

After visiting the poor at the house provided for their accommodation, and having a satisfactory meeting with the colored people, we parted with friends of Nantucket, and had a favored passage to New Bedford. In the evening we had a serious, and it is hoped a profitable meeting in this place.

Next day, the 10th of 6th month, we parted with our New Bedford Friends, and had a pleasant journey to New York, partly on the railroad, and partly by steamboat. In travelling at this amazingly rapid rate, my mind was forcibly struck with the vast difference between *our* getting along, and the travelling of our early Friends.

On seventh day evening we had a meeting at Friends' meeting-house on Downing street. Soon after it was gathered, a precious solemnity was felt; and during the testimony that I was led to deliver, this solemn feeling was happily increased; and such was the blessed effect that it seemed to embrace every mind present. I returned to my lodging rejoicing that Truth had reigned over all, and passed the night in sound, refreshing sleep.

13th.—First day morning, I attended Rose street meeting; in which I felt my mind opened to offer a small matter. But darkness seemed to thicken before me, and after saying a few words, I sat down, content to bear my own burden. After a few minutes, life arose; and with it a happy covering of humble confidence in the power of Truth, which gave an authority to proceed, and I delivered what was given me, to the relief of my own mind. In the afternoon I was at Hester street meeting, in which I had a favored opportunity; at the close of which I rejoiced because of the triumph of the great principle of Truth. The service was principally to urge the necessity of man's devotion to the manifestations of the light of the Spirit,—not only in great affairs, but also in matters by some held to be but small.

Next day I visited among my friends, and felt a particular satisfaction in the evidence of brotherly regard. The day following, Amos Willetts took us in his carriage to his father's, at Westbury on Long Island.

16th.—Attended Westbury Monthly Meeting; in which I had a testimony to deliver, which appeared to have a solemnizing effect, and I felt renewed in a blessed confidence in the guidance and government of the Divine Spirit. Next day we attended Jericho Monthly Meeting, which was a satisfactory opportunity; and I felt glad to observe the harmony prevailing among Friends. Lodged at Valentine Hicks's whose valuable wife is one of the daughters of the devoted Elias Hicks.

It is an important concern to visit the churches; and in passing through the service, there is great necessity to be watchfully on our guard; more especially in the present state of society. We now find that Friends have various views and modes of thinking, as to the duties we are called to : some think it is the duty of the society to mingle with other religious professors in promoting the cause—others believe that our preservation depends upon keeping separate, and minding our own business. For my part, I cannot think that we shall ever fulfill *our* duties, by getting into the mixture. It appears to me that the society has been much favored from its first rise, with the pure light of Truth ; and that in our solemn deliberations, it has often been our privilege to see that by dwelling alone we have maintained our strength, and have been favored to see what duties we are called to, and what subjects it has been best for us to let alone.

20th.—Had a meeting at Brooklyn, which was a precious opportunity. The sincere-hearted were encouraged, and the self-sufficient philosophers warned. In the evening I had a very large meeting in the city of New York ; in which my way opened to deliver a testimony, embracing a view of the importance of witnessing a subjection of the will of the creature to the will of the Creator. The testimony had a solemnizing effect : and I parted with Friends in much love.

Next day, we went on the steamboat, in the morning, and arrived in Philadelphia at one o'clock in the afternoon. On looking toward home, I felt a stop in my mind, and it appeared right that I should appoint two meetings in the city, if way opened for the same. But some Friends did not unite with this proposal.

22d.—This morning I felt at liberty to return home, where I arrived in the afternoon. It was cause of gratitude to feel my mind clothed with a peaceful quiet on my return. I also had much cause reverently to adore my merciful Creator for having furnished me with the needful help for every service unto which I was called.

When we are drawn from home in the service of Truth, it is a great favor to be permitted to see our way clearly from day to day, as we are passing along. But sometimes there are individuals who, from a particular desire that their meeting, or some other place should be visited, will try to urge the consideration of their proposals. By listening to the persuasions of such, the mind may become clouded; and thus the proper qualification to decide correctly may be lost, and the understanding involved in doubts.

When an instrument has been qualified to deliver a powerful and baptizing testimony, there are sometimes found those who extol him and thereby endanger his standing by raising in him a high opinion of his own qualifications. This applause of the instrument is always improper; and if the minister is not well guarded, may produce a very dangerous opinion of his own consequence.

27th.—On looking over the testimony of Margaret Fell concerning her husband, George Fox, it appeared from her account, that he was a man of constant devotion to the cause of God. In her view he was the first great instrument, raised up by the Divine Power to preach the everlasting gospel, after the dark night of apostacy that followed the days of the primitive church of Christ. Her testimony is a very clear one. But it would seem extraordinary, if the society of Friends in less than two hundred years should depreciate, and lose the life and power of religion, so as again to descend into a state of apostacy.

On the 20th of the 8th month, 1841, accompanied by Joseph S. Walton, and Abigail, his wife, I set out on a visit to some meetings and places in Lancaster county. That evening we lodged at Jesse Webster's.

On first day the 22d, in the morning, we attended Lampeter meeting, and I found the way open to deliver a testimony therein, and felt satisfied. In the afternoon I was at a meeting appointed in a neighborhood from among Friends. In it my spirit suffered under a sense of the want among the people, of being devoted to the gift of God in themselves; yet I was favored to deliver a very instructive testimony among them. My mind was in good measure relieved; though I could but mourn over the effect produced by an outward and formal ministry. Oh! saith my soul, when will the professors of the name of Christ, cease from man whose breath is in his nostrils? When will the inhabitants of the world come to rely alone upon that gospel which is preached in every creature, and which is the power of God unto salvation to all them that believe in and obey it! My spirit is grieved with the kind of preaching that is tolerated in the world, because I am sensible that much of it proceeds from that spirit that is cursed above every beast of the field. It seems to me that mankind are generally under and subject to the first, or animal nature; and that by the activity of this nature alone, they are led and moved in most of their professedly religious devotions. But all that can be gained by the wisest of those who are not subject to the eternal word of God, will end in disappointment and death; because it is not only by the power and influence of this living word, that the soul of man will ever be separated from the transgressing nature, and raised into the enjoyment of the favor of God.

After visiting some of our friends, we had a meeting at Bart on third day the 23d of the month. In this meeting my mind was again opened to bear a living testimony to the power and influence of the gift of God to man; showing that as the members of the primitive church stood faithful to this divine gift, the great cause of universal righteousness was advanced in the world. And that when the professed members of the church departed from the heavenly gift, the church lost its original standing, and darkness and superstition were introduced. If we of the present time are kept in the life and power of the gift of God, we must embrace it as our supreme teacher and director; for no other power or principle can ever redeem the soul of man, and give a qualification to enjoy the society of the blessed in the kingdom of God.

We lodged at Levi Pownal's, where I found the children respectful to their parents, and pleased with our company. I have often been in families where the conduct of the children has been very different. I believe it will always be found to be the case, that when they are taught a respectful obedience to their parents, they will be kindly disposed toward their friends.

24th.—We were at Sadsbury meeting, which was large for the place. In it my mind was much oppressed; but as I kept in the patient labor, life rose, and way opened for the delivery of an important testimony. I saw in the pure light that the state of the professors of the name of Christ, was generally one of great darkness ; and I reminded Friends of the ground occupied by the primitive believers ; and which, after a long night of apostacy and darkness, was again taken by our early Friends. I also held up the view, that the true light would again shine forth, and that many as from the four corners of the earth would be led by it, and thus be fitted to belong to that glorious company which John saw, that were gathered out of all nations, kindreds, tongues, and people. The meeting ended with solid comfort, and in the afternoon we had an agreeable ride home.

15th of the 10th month.—I was invited to attend the funeral of Isaac Smith's son. He died of a fever that has been prevailing in Chester county, and has taken off several blooming young persons. A large company of young people and others came together on this solemn occasion, and attended the meeting at London Grove. In this meeting, my mind was seriously impressed with the remembrance of that scripture testimony which states that all have sinned and fallen short of the testimony of the glory of God. I observed to the meeting, that I had no doubt this was a true testimony confirmed by the witness for God in every breast. It was therefore necessary that we should endeavor to have the burden of this condemnation removed before we go hence and are seen of men no more. A merciful God has provided the way and means of our deliverance from this burden, if we are willing to embrace the terms. He has declared by his prophet, that if we cease to do evil, and learn to do well,—though our sins have been of a deep dye, yet he will remove them, and love us freely. It was an opportunity to be remembered, and I returned home with the reward of peace.

On the 20th of the 10th month, 1841, I set out to attend Baltimore Yearly Meeting. On my way thither, I was at Deer Creek meeting, and we were favored with a comfortable solemnity. I was led to point out the necessity of being faithful to the Divine gift; and to show that in consequence of the unfaithfulness of some, the church was deprived of its dues. I saw that it was possible, when the day of account should come, to be in a state wherein the charge would be made, that "I was an hungered, and ye gave me no meat; I was thirsty, and ye gave me no drink," *&c.* The testimony appeared to make a deep and serious impression, and I was glad I had been with them. We lodged at John Jewett's; and next day rode to Baltimore. It was very comfortable to meet a number of valuable Friends, and I rejoiced to feel the prevalence of brotherly love among them.

While there, I felt an engagement to appoint a meeting in Lombard street house, at the west end of the city. It was a large meeting, in which the pure light and power of the gospel was livingly felt to be in dominion; and it might be said to be a memorable meeting. I had also a meeting appointed at the east end of the city, wherein I felt the power of truth to qualify for the service, and an important testimony was delivered. But the meeting appeared to be injured by communications that were consided as improper additions.

I attended most of the sittings of the Yearly Meeting, in which Friends were much favored with a precious covering of solemnity. Among the subjects brought before them was a proposal from one of the quarters to do away their tenth query. This case drew forth some instructive remarks on the danger of indulging in the society a disposition to be making changes, where no real necessity or advantage may require such a measure. During the time devoted to a consideration of this subject the minds of many Friends were profitably turned to reflect on the consequences which might justly be feared as the result of this changeable disposition. Some of the changes which have already been made, were adverted to; and it appears probable that in regard to some of them, Friends may yet see that it will be better to return to the old ground. This was held up to view in relation to that change of discipline which refers to the appointment of elders periodically. It is seriously doubted whether this alteration in regard to appointing elders has not been a loss to society much greater than any benefit that has yet arisen from the change.

In my best judgment upon the subject, I have never been prepared to unite with this measure; because I believe that no one can rightly be an elder in the church but such as are divinely gifted for the service. Now when the gifts of such are acknowledged by their being appointed to the station, to remove such from the service, or to limit the period of their standing in the office of elders, must be a loss, and no profit either to themselves or to the meetings. It produces unsettlement, and frequently consequences that tend to weaken the bonds of society.

On the 20th of the 8th month, 1842, I went, in company with Joseph S. Walton, on a visit to some of the meetings of Friends in Abington and Bucks Quarters. Next day we attended Darby meeting, which was a solemn opportunity; one in which I was favored to discharge my duty by delivering among them a plain testimony;—showing that all were blessed with the gift of the Divine Spirit, which was our all-sufficient teacher,—and that the nearer we kept to this guide, the more certain we should be of the perfection of its testimony. In the evening I attended a meeting appointed at Spruce street, Philadelphia; which though a season of favor to many, was very trying to my own mind.

Next day, we rode to Frankford, and had an evening meeting there. It was an opportunity in which I felt the power and light of Truth to be over all, and have abundant cause reverently to admire the mercy and goodness of God, in furnishing the necessary qualification to fulfill the service to which I was called, and by which the assembly were baptized into a state of great solemnity.

23d.—We went on to Samuel Comfort's, at the Falls, Bucks county, and next day attended the Quarterly Meeting of Ministers and Elders held there. In this meeting my mind was deeply exercised in support of our Christian testimony to the reality of the manifestation of the spirit of God in man, given to him as his all-sufficient guide from earth to heaven. It was, I thought, a profitable opportunity. The Quarterly Meeting for business next day, was a very trying time. The ministry was in the mixture, and there was a clashing and opposition manifested between two classes present. I felt best satisfied to remain silent. But it was clear to me that Friends will have to maintain the discipline by taking a decided stand against everything of the kind.

After the Quarterly Meeting was over, we went to Newtown, and put up with Joseph Briggs. On sixth day, the 26th, I had a meeting at Doylestown, and next day one at Plumstead. Then rode to John Watson's, at Buckingham, and attended a large and satisfactory meeting there. After having a meeting at Wrightstown on 2d day, the 29th of 8th month, we went by way of Newtown to Byberry, and were at the monthly meeting held there on 3d day. We next had an appointed meeting at Horsham, on fifth day the 1st of 9th month. Next day we rested at Joseph Foulke's and the day following had a meeting at Abington, which was large.

In the fall of the year 1844, in company with my valued friend, Joseph S. Walton, I visited the following named meetings: first, Huntington; next had a meeting at Petersburg, and then attended the Quarterly Meeting held at Huntington. Thence to Monallen, Pipe Creek, New Market, and Sandy Spring. Thence we went to Gunpowder, and attended Baltimore Quarterly Meeting held at that place. Thence to Little Falls, the Forrest, Fawn, and Broad Creek meetings. We then crossed the Susquehanna river, and were at Little Britain meeting, and thence home.

After being at home a short time, I again attended Baltimore Yearly Meeting, and had two appointed meetings after it concluded, both of which were satisfactory seasons. It is cause of humble gratitude that He that was my morning Light, has now in the evening of life given me strength to fulfil his will in the labors of the gospel.

1845, 20th of 2d month.—Having felt in my retired situation repeated evidences that Divine mercy has condescended to crown the evening of my life with the overflowings of his love, my mind has been led to consider the present state of the world, and to reflect upon what may be the probable events that may be expected to take place. From the present appearance of things there is much that goes to prove that the confidence of men in men is very much wanting. Hence there is reason to believe that great degrees of strife and contention will follow, the harmony and peace of families and neighborhoods be broken, and our country may be far removed from the quiet and happy condition that was enjoyed in the early settlement of it. It seems to me, that in a political point of view, the state we are in is a very unhappy one; divided into a number of parties, and much unkind feeling prevailing with many, which must have the effect of alienating the affections of one another, and hardening the heart. The various societies and associations that are formed for promoting particular objects, have too generally indulged a disposition to reflect on others who do not join with them, that they are quite as likely to do harm as good.

According to the observations I have made, and the views I have, I cannot believe that the world will be reformed by any other spirit than the peaceable spirit of the gospel of Christ. I am therefore a firm believer in his doctrine. Now he has said, "Whosoever gathereth not with me, scattereth abroad." Therefore, unless the minds of those who profess to be reformers are kept under the government of the heavenly gift of the Spirit of God, they will fail to improve the human family.

We have many persons going about our country, who are lecturing on various subjects; some on temperance, some on slavery, some on the doctrine of the peaceable spirit of Christ, &c. If those lecturers were under the solemn feelings of religious duty thus engaged, we might in that case expect some happy effects. But there is much reason to believe that many of them are acting from no higher or better motive than to have an employment of some degree of respectability, and to acquire applause, or pecuniary gain. These facts go to prove that their motives and their labors are very doubtful.

The subject of temperance is doubtless one of great value to mankind. It has for many years engaged the attention of the Society of Friends. When they became concerned to notice the use of distilled liquors in a society capacity, the article was common in nearly every family, and it was a general practice to have spirituous liquors in harvest fields. Very few farmers thought of gathering their hay and harvest without getting a quantity of spirits for daily use. It was also a very common practice to have a dram in the morning, almost the year through. The case is now very different. We seldom meet with it in any Friend's house. There is no necessity for Friends to be joining temperance societies. For the society of Friends is in itself a temperance society, on the principles of Christianity.

As to the subject of slavery—every man who has any just views of that subject, must be satisfied that it is a very great evil in our country,—and of course, must be desirous that the country should get clear of it without delay. But as it exists to a large amount,—particularly in the Southern States, it will require some time before it can be removed : and it is possible that by pressing the concern too hard, the evil may be prolonged, instead of hastening the period of its final termination. Taking a view of the state of the public mind, and comparing it with the means pursued by many for putting an end to slavery, there is some reason to fear, that they may result in a dreadful revolution. To my mind it is a clear case, that every cause must produce its own effect. If therefore, the public mind should become violently agitated by the parties opposed to each other, the danger might be that it might bring about a state of war and tumult.

4th month, 1845.—The circumstances of Friends as a religious society are such as to occasion many trials to a sincerely devoted mind. Instead of knowing our dependence to be placed on the government of the Divine Spirit, and waiting in all our proceedings for the renewed openings and light of Christ, our holy Head,—we too much depend on the powers of the human mind as men and creatures; and hence there is a lack of that deep and inward feeling after the mind of truth, which is necessary in order to come to a true judgment, in concerns that are brought before us; and thus, the animal nature takes the lead. The mind becomes separated from the spiritual life, and darkness is felt to spread over our meetings. Hence, there is not that unity and harmony in society, which was formerly experienced; nor are the proceedings and conclusions of society marked with the weight and clearness that once prevailed.

But notwithstanding these evidences of weakness and dereliction of principle in too many, there are still preserved some living members in our meetings generally. There is therefore ground to hope that Zion may yet arise and shake herself not only from the dust of the earth, but from all defilements of flesh and spirit, and come forward in her original dignity and beauty, clothed with the sun and the moon under her feet, and a crown of twelve stars upon her head.

In considering the present state of society, I have had my attention turned to look at the causes which have contributed to its decline from the ground it once occupied. Among these causes this view has presented: Formerly, in the institution of our meetings for discipline, those members only were permitted a seat in them who were of orderly life and conversation, and who had a religious concern for the maintenance of our Christian testimonies,—all others were excluded as not being suitable to compose meetings for discipline. These meetings being thus composed of solid, exemplary and experienced Friends, were the means of rendering them useful and preserving them in a state of greater solemnity and feeling after the mind of Truth in all their proceedings and conclusions. The unity and harmony of society was thus promoted and maintained,—the health, the welfare, and the preservation of the body, were the objects of the godly care of the elders and livingly concerned members of the church.

It may readily be conceived that when Yearly, Quarterly, and Monthly Meetings, were composed of this description of members only, that they were very different both in their character and effects, from our present meetings of discipline. Now it appears to me that the time is at hand for the society of Friends to return to its first principles in relation to these institutions. It is time for rightly-concerned Friends to seek after the mind of Truth, in regard to the maintenance of order, and the exercise of Christian discipline, on the original ground that George Fox moved on in the setting up of meetings for the discipline of the church.

On the 9th of the 9th month, 1845, I mentioned to our Monthly Meeting, that my mind was impressed, for the first time in my life, with a concern to make a visit to the families of Friends, and, in this case it was to Friends of Kennett Monthly Meeting. The concern was considered and fully united with.

On first day, the 14th, I attended Marlborough meeting. During this opportunity my mind was brought into a feeling sense of the dependent state of man ; and I could see clearly that of ourselves we can do nothing. After meeting I went home with William Barnard, and after dinner we proceeded together in the proposed family visit, and had religious opportunities in four families.

Thence we continued from day to day to prosecute the concern, and I felt my way open to offer such remarks and communicate such matter for the consideration of those whom we visited, as were from time to time furnished me. I also attended the regular meetings as they came in course, and they were instructive opportunities.

Here the journal, left by Jesse Kersey, ceases—that portion of it which details the particulars of his visit to England is one penned long afterwards, and is said to be much inferior in interest to another written at or about the time of the journey. To recover this account the publication of the present volume has been considerably delayed, but, after many fruitless efforts, it is believed to have been irretrievably lost.

ESSAYS AND LETTERS.

As the rise of the Society of Friends was an occurrence of a very extraordinary character, and attended with circumstances which prove the aid of Almighty power, and the presence of unlimited wisdom, it has appeared to me to be among the events that are worthy of particular attention. I shall therefore attempt to bring into view such cases as appear to me to be of vast importance to the world of mankind, in relation to the objects they were calculated to promote, when rightly understood and practically adopted.

It must be admitted as a remarkable circumstance, that an individual should succeed, as was the fact in the case of George Fox, in changing the order of a powerful government on the subject of oaths. When he took up this testimony to truth-speaking, and absolutely determined, let the consequences be what they might, never to swear in any case, he stood alone in this concern. Magistrates, judges, and lawyers were all against him. To them it appeared to be an attack upon the whole judiciary system. The general apprehension was that oaths could not be dispensed with; that they were always necessary in taking evidence upon actions in law. It was insisted on that evidence in courts must be given under oath—how else could it be credited? It would therefore never do to let any visionary reformer lay waste the use of oaths. The doctrine preached by an unlettered man on this subject must not be permitted to obtain credit, and therefore he must be opposed.

Here, then, we find the conflict to commence. George Fox brings the question of oaths to the single point—whether to obey Christ or man. Jesus Christ had said, "Swear not at all," but the civil power says you must swear; I cannot obey both. Which then shall I obey? George Fox makes his choice, and determines to obey Christ as the Saviour of men. He cannot believe that the testimony against oaths is an evil. But he is convinced that what Christ commanded must be right, and that therefore the world must be reformed on this subject. Under these views George Fox commenced and maintained his testimony against swearing. We therefore find him uniformly firm in the support of his belief, that it would be a sin for him to swear. And when the officers of the government administered to him the oath, he would tell them that he had never taken an oath in his life, and that his Saviour had commanded him not to swear. This was his uniform practice; and generally he was sent to jail, where he would remain until the way was made for him to come out again, without compromising his testimony. At Lancaster he was brought before the court, and the judge ordered him to take the oath of allegiance to the king, commanding the book to be given him. When he had received the book, he opened it at the passage where Christ commanded not to swear at all; and holding up the Bible in the court, he thus remarked: "You have commanded me to swear, and have given me a book that says, 'Swear not at all.'" Determining to do as the book directed, George would not swear, and of course was sent to prison, from which in process of time he was released.

Thus it was with George Fox, until by his firm and unwavering testimony against swearing, many were convinced of the truth of his doctrine, and brought to embrace the christian testimony against taking oaths in any case whatever. The government at length so far gave up the matter, as to make a law by which an affirmation should be accepted instead of an oath.

Here, then, we may see that a single individual, by continuing faithful to the testimony unto which he was called, became the great instrument of converting a nation to the admission of a more correct practice.

Having settled the principle of speaking the truth, and letting our yea be yea, and our nay, nay, and thus determined that all oaths were unnecessary and unlawful to those who obey the command of Christ, George Fox found in his devotion to the openings of the Divine Spirit, that the worship and ministry which obtained in England was outward and formal, and that the people were led to trust the great concern of the soul's salvation to a mere formal acknowledgment of some of the doctrines of the apostles and primitive christians, without experiencing the fulfillment of them in their own minds. He was therefore impressed with a belief that it was his duty to proclaim everywhere that the Lord had come to teach his people himself, and to call them off from a dependence on the teachings of men; that Christ Jesus was the true light which enlightens every man that cometh into the world, and therefore, if they would come to Christ, they must cease to depend upon man, whose breath is in his nostrils. He also declared that the ministry of Christ was free; that the true worship was spiritual, and that the church of Christ was made up of living members, a spiritual and heavenly church, not made with hands, as their steeple houses were. He further held forth among the people that their ministry was a false ministry, and their steeple houses were idols; that their worship was not spiritual but formal, and therefore of no value in the sight of God.

In the preaching of George Fox, there was a baptizing power attended him, which took a deep hold on the minds of the people, and many were convinced thereby; so that in a few years many fellow believers were gathered unto him, and came forth in the promulgation of the same simple and blessed doctrines.

Not only was George Fox abundantly persecuted and calumniated through the instigation of the priests, being frequently imprisoned, as well as beaten and abused by the populace, but those also who became fellow-believers with him were subjected to the same kind of sufferings; some being made and kept prisoners for years, and much of their property seized and taken from them, for fines and penalties imposed upon them. But no power on earth could turn those early converts from the faith they had in the divine gift, which they felt in themselves, and which they knew was sufficient to direct and support their minds under every trial. According to the history concerning them, as given by William Sewel, it is manifest that as they were persuaded they were led by the Spirit of God, so they were supported by him. And it would seem that nothing short of the preserving power of God could have sustained and kept them in the wonderful manner in which they were supported under the severe trials they met with from the priests and governments of that day. The priests in particular were violent against them, because, as they said, they were a people that increased in all parts of the nation, and not only those of the middle and lower ranks among the people united with them, but that not a few of those who were men of rank, and of the first talents and standing, joined themselves to this society. They were therefore alarmed, and doubted what this profession might come to. It seemed from their rapid increase, and from the love and friendship that was among them, as if they might in time triumph over them altogether. Such opinions did take place in England, for we find that great man Admiral Penn, when on his death-bed held sentiments of this kind. Calling his son William to his bed side when near his close, he said to him, "Son William, if you and your friends keep to your plain way of living, and your plain way of preaching, you will make an end of the priests to the end of the world." It was partly from fears and apprehensions of this kind, that Friends in the beginning were sorely persecuted.

Contemplating the rise of this people, and how admirably they were supported and carried through those severe trials and persecutions, it is obvious that nothing short of divine power could have given them the capacity and strength, the patience and fortitude to endure it all, and come out in the end such a respectable and important society of people. What other power could they lean upon, when the strong arm of the civil government was raised against them? It is from a conviction that the Lord only was their support, their guide and protector, that I am of the judgment that Friends were brought into being for the purpose of gaining to the great cause of christianity some important advancement in the world. Already they have been the great instrumental means of teaching mankind the doctrine of the sovereign rights of conscience. By their sufferings they have maintained this doctrine, and proved that the mind of man when brought into submission and conformity to the gift of God cannot be subdued by any earthly power; that as men come under the obligations and influence of Christian principles, it is vain for any earthly power to attempt to compel them to bend to a different course, or to induce them to adopt a different practice. It is therefore obvious that Friends have been the means of establishing those principles, and that no human government can triumph over the enlightened conscience. Hence we may conclude that Friends have only to conform to their religious profession, and live up to the principles of Truth, and they must convince the world that conscience is the sovereign right of the Almighty, and must be left free.

The society of Friends have not only held up to view the sacred rights of conscience, but they are also persuaded that the same divine power and principle which raised up George Fox and his fellow-laborers, has given them a number of testimonies to advance in the world. These testimonies and views they believe must obtain, and will ultimately triumph over all opposition. Among these important discoveries of the light of divine truth, stands conspicuous the testimony to the free ministry of the gospel, in opposition to a hireling or paid ministry. Friends believe that this testimony can never be suffered to fall to the ground, but will continue and increase until it shall (according to

Admiral Penn's prediction) make an end of the priests to the end of the world.

In the rising and spreading of Truth, the society of Friends were called upon to advocate and maintain a testimony to the equal and general right of all men to freedom. In attending to this righteous concern, the Society has set an example to the rest of mankind. For although at one period they held slaves among them, yet through patient, persevering labor they became separated from this evil; and for many years past, no person can hold slaves, and at the same time be a member of the Society.

The Society has also a testimony against contention, wars, and fightings; and no member can take part in any of the military measures resorted to by the government. But in all the wars and fightings that occur they must stand separate, and take no part in any thing of the kind. They know that Christ, the Prince of peace has said that his kingdom is not of this world; for if his kingdom were of this world, then would his servants fight.

The society of Friends having been raised up by the power of the Almighty, and marvellously protected and preserved, it would seem extraordinary if they should be permitted to fall away, and cease to be useful in the great family of mankind. And yet this must be the case, if it should fail to answer the important end for which it has been raised up in the world. It would not be reasonable to suppose that the light with which we have been blest, and the important testimonies that have been given us to bear,—have been exclusively for our own sake: and if there is cause to conclude that our existence as a people has been with a view of our being useful to others, it is then highly necessary that we should continue faithful to the light that has been given us. The testimony to the spirituality of the Christian religion, stands eminent among those with which we are furnished ;—because it is clear that if the great end of the coming of Christ was to establish a religion upon the doctrine of the immediate revelation of the spirit of God to the soul of man, (and this appears to be one of the principles in regard to which we stand alone, or differ from most others) it must be evident that the maintenance of this fundamental doctrine is one of the main points for which we have a being. It is therefore the duty of the society to watch against everything that would tend to lead off from faithfully supporting this testimony.

Now if we judge of effects from their predisposing causes, there is no step the society could take that would be more likely to become a cause of the loss of this testimony, than that of joining with those who reject this doctrine,—and proceeding with them into actions and measures professedly for advancing moral and religious concerns. Because, when we unite with others who do not credit the belief that a divine guide is furnished to man, and proceed with them to act on important concerns, without waiting for the direction and influence of the spirit of truth, we are evidently departing from our own proper ground,—a dependence on divine revelation. For, contrary to this belief in divine revelation, those with whom we thus associate generally maintain the opinion that their own reason, understanding and natural faculties or talents, are a sufficient guide, and any further or higher qualification is not to be expected.

Now the society of Friends may be considered as a people chosen for the support of the doctrines of the divine gift to man as his own safe leader in every step he takes. Therefore, the pursuit of any object which in any measure dispenses with the necessity of waiting for the divine manifestation in man,—appears to be dangerous and should be carefully avoided by Friends. It is cause of concern to find our members connecting themselves with others of the class above alluded to, for the purpose of advancing any of our religious testimonies. For, however sincere they may apprehend themselves to be, there is reason to believe that such will in the end balk the great testimonies of truth, and fall away from the only safe ground, on which the upright maintenance of our religious principles, and our Christian testimonies can be rightly supported, and the cause of universal righteousness advanced in the world.

ON PRAYER.

It appears to me that this important concern is not correctly estimated by many professors of religion; and therefore on entering into the act, they lose sight of the advice of the Saviour upon this awful subject. It appears clear, that he encouraged his disciples to live in a state of prayer,—that they should always cherish in their minds, desires for the blessings of preservation; and therefore has promised that if we ask, we shall receive. Now it is evident if no request is made, there can be no reason to expect that anything will be granted. But those precious souls who are quickened by an experimental knowledge of the love of God, are always leaning upon, and looking to the divine spirit for preservation ; and therefore they ask in agreement with the mind of the spirit, and that which they ask for they receive.

But although such are the blessed privileges of the saints, yet it may be taken for granted, that in the multitude of expressions used by many in the form of prayer, it is in reality not such, and therefore will not be granted. In the sixth chapter of Matthew the Saviour has furnished such views of this subject as every Christian should seriously examine and consider. He charges the Pharisees with loving to pray standing at the corners of the streets, that they might be seen of men. He also remarked that they made use of many words; as if the great giver of every good and perfect gift required to be informed of what we stood in need of. On this point he tells us that our Father knoweth what we stand in need of before we ask him. He therefore recommends us to make our prayers in secret; and assures us that our Father who sees in secret, himself will reward us openly. As I have reflected upon this subject, I have been convinced that it is time for a reform to take place in relation to it.

Many meetings are held that go under the name of *prayer meetings;* and in them the persons composing them are in the practice of what they call praying, one after another. So far as I can understand the subject, it would be improper for the different members to repeat their request for the same thing. If one person is authorized to pray in a meeting, his prayer is offered on behalf of all that are present. And it appears like a repetition, for another to put up his request in the same meeting for the same thing.

By prayer, I understand that the individual solicits that the will of God may be done. Any other request must be contrary to the Divine Mind, and therefore could not be acceptable to the Almighty, nor can we believe that it would be granted. Prayer, therefore, to be acceptable to God, must be dictated by the Divine Spirit. Consequently all those who attempt to pray without being moved thereunto by the Divine Spirit are acting in their own wills, and cannot be thereby benefited.

In my reflections upon this subject I have been led to desire that in the society of Friends especially, as we profess to be a spiritually-minded people, we may be very guarded how we undertake to call an assembly into the solemn act of vocal supplication, upon any outward natural feeling, or consideration. In my own experience, I may say, that I have found, when I have felt something moving on my mind and seeming to point to a public act, that as I have calmly waited for a clear opening to move therein, the impression has subsided and settled away; and the mind has been released by an inward and spiritual application to the throne of grace. It is this kind of prayer that is evidently recommended by the blessed Saviour of men. Surely, if when we pray, we are to enter into the closet and shut the door,—we are then waiting upon our holy Head, and he will, according to his promise, reward us openly.

ON THE MINISTRY.

It has been the opinion of Friends, that the great Creator of man is the sovereign Lord of conscience. In accordance with this opinion, if any member believes that he or she is called to the work of the ministry, such have a right to offer their communications in our meetings; and after hearing them, Friends are to judge whether they have received a gift in the ministry or not. In fulfilling this duty great care should be exercised not to admit into the mind any prejudice against the individual so appearing, lest we should be thereby prompted to throw discouragements in the way of a tender and rightly-exercised mind, and thus hinder him or her from coming forward, as might have been the case had he or she been properly or tenderly treated. For it sometimes happens that the great Head of the church, in calling his exercised children to the ministry, requires of them only the expression of a few words; and these appearing very simple, Friends who judge only by the strength of the natural understanding, may condemn or not approve them,—when the appearance has been the fruit of pure obedience to a Divine call. In such case the poor minister may be at a loss how to get along; when he feels in himself an approving conscience for what he has done, but finds his friends are dissatisfied. In this close trial, if the individual sincerely believes that he is called to appear in the ministry, and the officers of the church tell him he had better be quiet, he had better be silent; because the instrument can be under no obligation to speak, where there are none to hear. But there may be a want of qualification to hear and to judge correctly,—as well as to speak. Where the defect may be in the hearers, it may be thought to be oppression, under these circumstances, to silence the speaker. But I do not consider that to be the case: because the speaker is to lay by for a time only, and this may be profitable for his deepening in the root of life; for by this submission to his Friends, he is not to consider himself acquitted from the concern, but merely held as a probationer for a season, and may come forward again when he feels the weight of the Divine call renewed. Thus, harmony and unity and peace may be preserved, and the right thing in due time take place.

THE church of Christ is one body, the members of which live under the government of the same Head, and are bound by their allegiance to him to maintain the same important testimonies. Hence, a question arises whether, in the present divided state of the Society of Friends,* those who are of one heart and of one soul are not kept more distinct and separate than they should be in the right order of things? If this is found to be the case,—and if in unity there is strength, what is the part we are called upon to act in our present condition? I am of the judgment that it is time for something to be done that might lead to a reunion of the society of Friends.

It has been a settled opinion in my mind, that our religious society has not been raised up and rendered conspicuous in the world exclusively for our own

* Alluding to the separation of 1827.

sakes; but on the contrary, that we were intended to be as lights in the world—as a city set on a hill that cannot be hid. We have been called to hold up testimonies of great magnitude, and they are still required to be maintained. Our testimony to a free gospel ministry, which is opposed to a ministry brought forth in the will and contrivance of the natural man,—is not among the least; nor is our testimony to the nature of that spiritual worship which is acceptable to the divine mind. These, as well as various other testimonies which we have been called to bear, are of vast importance to ourselves and to the world of mankind.

Considering those facts, it has been to me an instructive, as well as humbling circumstance, to witness the simultaneous and awful shaking which has taken place in all parts of the society; and I have been ready to conclude it was just such a shaking and overturning as we stood in need of. And it may even yet be that a still more awful and solemn overthrow is to follow. For what can we say has been the effect of the shaking and agitation we have had? Has it been the means of humbling us, and bringing us back to the original ground and fundamental principle of our profession? Or rather is it not obvious that too much formality, indifference, and self-importance remain, and have even increased among us?

Instead of being humbled, and recurring to first principles, and to our first love, are we not building again those very things which are to be taken down—joining hands with formal professors, and saying, "See how they are coming over to us; witness their zeal in forming temperance societies, and in our testimony against slavery." But did the will and contrivance of the natural man ever work the righteousness of God? Verily nay; it never did, and never will. If we look back to Friends in the beginning, it is manifest that they were led by the Divine Spirit in carrying on the works of righteousness, and bearing a faithful testimony to the Truth. But the world and the priests persecuted them, and were very far from owning them or their doctrines and testimonies. Have we any reason to believe that the spirit of the natural, unregenerate man is in any degree different now from what it was then? Certainly not any. And therefore if the preservation of a pure testimony to the way and work of God's salvation now is the same as it was in the beginning, it must be evident that those who are joining with the spirit of the world are departing from the true ground and foundation, and are entering into connection with that which is no better than idolatry. For other foundation can no man lay than that which is already laid, Jesus Christ, the righteous. Hence we may infer that as respects the principles of the society of Friends, the stir and noise that is being made in the world, are only the products of that spirit which is "cursed above every beast of the field." It is therefore highly needful for Friends to have their eyes opened, and to see where they are going, and what they are doing. For if the cause of God and the advancement of his kingdom is promoted in the earth, it must be by his own Spirit alone, and not another.

If the foregoing views are correct, it is high time for the members of our Society to be awakened, and to recur to first principles; for it is certain that if we depart from the Divine Guide, and connect ourselves with those who do not believe in the testimony and influence of this precious gift, there will be on our part a falling away from the Truth,—and the spirit of antichrist will gain the ascendency. I am abundantly convinced that it is not in the wisdom or talents of the natural man merely to see into the path of divine appointment, nor can the mere wisdom and contrivance of the creature ever promote the great and glorious cause of the all-wise Creator.

Hence I feel it as a duty to leave this testimony behind me, to the absolute necessity that exists for the Society of Friends to maintain their profession and practical belief in the only sure and saving principle of divine wisdom given to man for his guide into all Truth. And I am persuaded that as we come home to this heavenly ground and abide on this safe and solid foundation, the great body of Friends will continue to be made use of by our holy Head in advancing the blessed kingdom and government of Christ on the earth. But should we suffer ourselves to be beguiled and led away from the sure foundation, and thus join in with measures pursued by the carnal wisdom and will of the natural man, we shall fall away from our proper standing, and shall wither and dwindle from the life and power of the gospel. It is therefore my ardent concern to call all my dear friends every where, to come out of Babylon, and touch not the unclean thing. Then He that was the morning light of the Society, and by whose light and power Friends were marvelously directed and preserved, will continue to be our leader, our guide, and our preserver, in safety and in peace, to our great consolation, and to the glory of his ever excellent name.

ON WAR.

It has been my lot to be frequently engaged in defence of the peaceable principles of the Christian religion. During the last war with Great Britain, I felt a concern to go to Washington, in order to try to prevail with our rulers to embrace the first opening to close the contest. When there, I first called on James Madison, the President of the United States, and mentioned to him how affecting it was to contemplate the condition of the inhabitants along the frontiers of our country, exposed as they were to the sound of the instruments of death. He seemed to feel the weight of my concern for the return of peace to our land. I had also an opportunity with James Monroe, then Secretary of State. I found him surrounded with a large company of gentlemen and ladies, as they are usually called. The company seemed to look upon us as out of place, and some of them smiled upon our appearance and manners. But while I was opening my concern, particularly in relation to the afflicted inhabitants along the frontiers of our country, I observed several of those called ladies who shed tears. The Secretary handed me a printed sheet of paper, which he said would show me the justness of our cause. I remarked that I would look over it; but before leaving the subject I would mention a case that had occurred between two wealthy and high spirited men. They had unhappily misunderstood each other, and a quarrel ensued. Such were their high-toned feelings of animosity that all that could be done to reconcile them seemed to be without effect. It happened, however, that these two men were one day riding out, each in his own carriage, and about to meet in the road. The one thought he would not turn out, and the other determined on the same course. But when they were coming near to each other, one of them reflected that it would be a shameful business to break down in the public road, when there was ample room for them to pass without coming in collision. With these thoughts he told his driver to turn out. The other then said if the first had not turned out, he intended to do so. In this case he that first gave way acted the most honorable part, while the other could make but a poor acknowledgment. Now here is the difficulty. Men are commonly too self-willed, and will not yield as they should do when provocation or disputes, real or imaginary, occur, and thus it is that quarrels and wars are commenced and carried on with a vindictive spirit. The secretary confessed that such was human nature, and that hence it was that wars were continued in the world.

ON THE FORMS OF WORSHIP AMONG FRIENDS.

It has been very judiciously remarked, "That no form of meeting together for the purpose of Divine worship could be more perfect than that of meeting together in silence: and therefore it was impossible to make any improvement upon this form." Now this "form of meeting" is intended as an introduction to the "substance" of the figure used by Jesus Christ in relation to the spirituality of all acceptable worship. After cautioning his disciples against the formality and many words of the hypocrites he says. "But thou when thou prayest, enter into thy closet, and when thou hast shut the door, pray to thy Father which is in secret." "And when ye pray, use not vain repetitions, as the heathen do."

But the perfection of the outward form of meeting together in silence, is subject also to the act of vocal preaching and vocal prayer, for the purposes of mutual comfort, instruction and edification.

In accordance with what are considered apostolic views of the forms connected with preaching and praying, the person who believes him or herself Divinely called vocally to preach or to pray in a meeting uncovers the head in testimony of reverence to the Divine Fountain whence all true gospel preaching and acceptable prayer proceeds. To this form of uncovering the head in time of public vocal supplication, is added that of kneeling, as the expression of humble and reverential feeling in thus approaching the throne of grace, and addressing the Majesty of heaven. The company, or assembly present on this solemn occasion also rise, and the men uncover their heads in token of reverence to the Divine Being thus vocally addressed in their hearing, by one professing to be Divinely moved thereunto.

These views of the subjects of Divine worship, gospel ministry, and public vocal prayer, appear to be consonant with the principles and practice of the primitive Christians, and those of our early Friends, such as George Fox, Robert Barclay, William Penn, and other faithful Friends in that day, and ever since down to the present time.

Ever since the year 1719, our Discipline has contained the substance of the following conclusion and judgment of the body. "As the occasion of our religious meetings is solemn, a care should ever be maintained to guard against anything that would tend to disorder or confusion therein. When any think they have aught against what is publicly delivered, they should speak to the party privately and orderly; and if any shall oppose a ministering Friend who is in unity and not disowned by any meeting, in his or her preaching or exhortation, or keep on the hat, or show any other remarkable dislike to such in time of prayer,—let them be speedily admonished as disorderly persons who endanger the peace and oppose the charity and brotherhood of the church."

In this clause of the Discipline and regulation of society, the keeping on of the hat in time of public vocal supplication appears to refer to cases of "dislike" toward the individual thus engaged. But there are and have been those who keep their seats, and keep on the hat, in time of vocal prayer, when no dislike or disunity is felt toward the person so engaged. And among these are found such as plead a conscientious scruple as the ground of their not conforming to this long-established order and custom. This plea of conscience appears to arise from the mistaken motive of considering the custom of rising and taking off the hat, as intended to express unity with what is uttered in vocal prayer, or unity and respect or reverence toward the individual praying. But the origin of the custom had no further reference to the person supplicating, than a belief of his or her being, or professing to be immediately called to this duty, and Divinely qualified to perform it.

Now the Yearly Meeting and the society of Friends

from the beginning appear to have considered the "form" of rising and uncovering the hèad during the time of vocal supplication in our public meetings, as tending to the solemnity and right order of those religious opportunities: and therefore provision is made in the Discipline in order to guard against everything that may "tend to disorder or confusion therein." But on such solemn occasions, for some to stand up and uncover the head, and others to keep their seats with their hats on has the appearance of "disorder," and tends to the "confusion" of young and tender minds, who are unable to account for this diversity of practice.

Considering the simple form of rising and taking off the hat, as having been adopted by the society on the principle of its being an appropriate expression of reverence to the Divine Being on the occasion of his being thus vocally and publicly addressed, it seems difficult to assign any just cause of a conscientious difficulty in the case with any one. No one is injured by it—and if the act takes place merely in submission to the judgment and established order of the society, it cannot harm any one to comply with the custom. But it may promote an essential benefit to ourselves and others, to conform to this solemn order from the principle and feeling of reverence and love to our heavenly Father,—and may tend to the harmony, peace and satisfaction one of another.

THE society of Friends as a distinct body of Christian professors, appears to have been raised up for great and special purposes, and to be as lights in the world of mankind. Hence in the early rise of the society, we find by their history that Friends were called to maintain testimonies to the Christian religion which were different from those of other professors ; and yet were consonant with the scriptures and with the doctrines of Christ and his apostles. Among these important testimonies was that in relation to the spirituality of Divine worship. They believe that as " God is a Spirit," so the worship that is acceptable to him must also be spiritual. They believed also that " God is love," and therefore that all true worshippers must dwell in love, agreeably to the command of Christ. They likewise believed that God had come to teach his people himself, by the light of his own spirit in their hearts. Hence, as they found the profession and manner of worship among the different sects of professors, to be outward and formal, under the influence of a mercenary priesthood, they were induced to withdraw from them and hold their meetings in silent waiting upon God, unless some were called to minister of the free gift of the gospel to the people.

For their faithful maintenance of this testimony to the public, social, and spiritual worship of Almighty God, they underwent severe trials and persecutions, being often stoned, mobbed, and dragged out of their meetings, at the instigation of the priests. They were also fined, imprisoned, and many were spoiled of their substance, and died in noisome jails and dungeons. But nothing could shake their confidence, or divert them from the performance of this reasonable duty, when at liberty and in health. Hence, when they were debarred from entering their meeting houses, by an armed force, or when these were demolished by the rude mobs,—they would meet in the streets or on the ruins, as near the appointed place as they could—such was their love one to another, and such was their zeal for the support of this righteous testimony that the declarations made by one of them to their persecutors, seemed applicable to them all—" You might as well think to hinder the sun from shining, or the tide from flowing, as to think to hinder the Lord's people from meeting to wait upon him, whilst but two of them are left together."

But what shall be said now in this day of outward ease and liberty? Is this testimony to the public and spiritual worship of our Almighty Benefactor, of less importance to individuals, and to the world of mankind, than it was formerly? Surely not. Then how is it that our religious meetings are neglected by so large a portion of those who consider themselves as members of the same society, and profess the same principles and testimonies, that our predecessors did? This delinquency is complained of from year to year, in the Reports of the state of society carried up to almost every Yearly Meeting from its constituent branches. Not only is this neglect continued from year to year, embracing a large portion of our members, more especially in relation to meetings held near the middle of the week; but a considerable number wholly neglect all our meetings; and another class of members, some of whom may be said to occupy conspicuous stations in society, do not hesitate to express their doubts of the usefulness of our religious meetings, and hold up the view that people may be as good at home.

Such being the present state of the society of Friends, it may well be queried whether we are the same people, holding the same principles, testimonies and views as were practically held and manifested by early Friends. It is evident that very many who claim a right of membership in the society are deficient in the practice of a due attendance of our religious meetings; and hence they fail of this evidence in support of the important testimony to the public worship of the Father of spirits. Social worship embraces the doctrine and principle of brotherly love. Must it therefore be inferred that those who neglect to attend meetings for worship, are deficient in love to their brethren.

But, without entering into inquiries after the causes of delinquency, the fact is obvious and certain. And while this continues to be the state and condition of the society it cannot, in relation to this and other important testimonies, be as a light to the world, and a useful body in spreading the pure doctrines of the gospel among mankind. It therefore appears highly needful for livingly-concerned Friends to seek for Divine wisdom and right ability in the exercise of Christian discipline toward those members who neglect the due attendance of our religious meetings. We know there must be a defect of principle in these delinquents, and that they do not conform to the precepts and examples of our primitive Friends, or of the early Christians. Among the apostles, and the righteous in all ages, there appears to have been a living concern on this subject. They were convinced of the rectitude and benefit of frequently assembling together for the solemn purpose of Divine worship and mutual comfort and edification. Paul besought his brethren by the high and holy object of the mercies of God, that they would present their bodies as living sacrifices, holy and acceptable unto God; and this he declared to be their reasonable service.

So far as we have the evidence of facts and observation in relation to this subject, it goes to prove that those who neglect this important duty, seldom advance in their love to the Supreme or to their fellow creatures —but on the contrary, are deficient in the due support of other Christian testimonies. Thus, they fall away from the precious guidance of the Spirit of Truth in themselves;—they are not alive in the love of God and of the brotherhood, and their delinquency gives evidence of it; for where this love abounds in the heart, it leads those who possess it to love to be often together, and to enjoy the benefits of public social worship. Hence we infer that those who neglect the attendance of our religious meetings, are lacking in the great Christian principle of love in themselves, and therefore they do not feel it toward others.

Now when a member of our society has let go this fundamental in religion, and given up the practice of attending meeting with his friends,—if after patient and continued labors for his restoration, he remains still negligent,—there can be no further use in his being continued a member of the society: but there may be, and doubtless often is a great injury and disadvantage sustained. For while the society permits such delinquent members to continue violating or disregarding the important testimony of Truth, and the vital principles on which it exists, this connivance is noticed by others, and they are induced to conclude that while a person may be continued a member, and yet fail or be negligent in such important testimonies and consistency of conduct,—there is little or no advantage in being a member of such a society. Hence, sincere seeking minds may be discouraged, and a stumbling block be thrown in their way, by continuing those unsound members among us.

Again, much disadvantage may arise, and weakness and declension ensue,—where individuals who neglect the attendance of our religious meetings, particularly near the middle of the week, and yet are regular in most other respects,—are appointed to services in society, or placed in the station of clerks, overseers and other offices. Now it is obvious, that when a monthly meeting sanctions the appointment of such delinquent members, it is a tacit acknowledgment that such meeting is in a state of weakness, and connives at the violation of the testimonies of truth in or by its members. Such a monthly meeting evidently needs the supervisory care of its quarterly meeting. It may be stated that in all cases where the testimonies and principles of truth as professed by the society of Friends, are violated, or the judgment and conclusions of the Body disregarded by any of our members and this is known to be the fact, such individuals should be called to account, and labored with in the spirit of meekness and love, in order for their restoration—and if such labor should prove ineffectual, and the offender will not submit to the sense and advice of his friends, the use and benefit of society to such an one being thus at an end, it would be better for society and also for the refractory member, that a separation should take place and a minute of disownment be issued.

The Lamb and his followers shall have the victory; and that victory is not the result of temporal or carnal resistance; for all they that take the sword shall perish with the sword: but it is a victory gained by patient suffering,—by non-resistance. For those who make no resistance can never be conquered; they may be persecuted and turned out of temporal existence, but they cannot be destroyed. Those who say they are the disciples of Christ ought to remember that their Lord has said, "Ye are not of this world, for I have chosen you out of the world, that ye should bring forth much fruit. If ye were of the world, the world would love its own; but because I have chosen you out of the world, therefore doth the world hate you." And, "the friendship of this world is enmity with God" —and "the wisdom of this world is foolishness with God." How then can the disciple of Christ join hands with contending elements! Let not any be deceived who have known the Truth. If the Truth make you free, then are ye free indeed. All the powers of darkness, and every thing that makes opposition, that leans to or calculates upon human power, will in the end be subdued; and the Lamb of God who taketh away the sin of the world,—having wearied out all opposition, and established his kingdom by entreaty,—it alone shall stand. But every other kingdom and power shall have an end. They form the means for their own destruction,—they lean upon the sword, and consequently perish.

Thus it has been through many generations, and

thus it will continue to be with every compulsive system. But the peculiar glory of the Divine government stands in its unconquerable forbearance. How then can those who say they are called to show forth this kingdom, and to witness that it has come in their hearts, be shaken in mind, or turned in any manner to lean upon the policy of nations? Why should they be disturbed by any of the jarring powers of the earth? Ought they not as passive spectators placed upon an eminence, to let the tumults pass by,—rather than sink into the throng of contention?

Under these considerations, I have had a weighty concern on my mind; and as I have endeavored to keep my standing in the unchangeable Truth, I have seen that if my fellow-professors, who I believe are called upon in these latter ages to hold up the true Light, do not keep to the pure foundation they will be driven from the oracle of God, and will be left to stumble and fall in the darkness of human measures and human policy. Under these impressions it has opened in prospect to endeavor to give forth a watch-word, and to call upon those who are in danger of being led away,—to return to the Rock of ages,—abide in their tents,—beware how they suffer their spirits to be allied to any of those who are leaning upon a contrary principle. Every species of reasoning about civil government and its uses or importance, I believe I have found has a tendency to draw the mind from the proper foundation, and will, in its effect, weaken the confidence of those who indulge in it, and lessen their dependence upon the Divine Power. But, dear friends, if we believe that we are called upon to be examples of the believers, how shall we comply with this duty, unless we manifest in times of trial a holy dependence upon the Head of the church! Has there ever been a day when the disciples of Christ were authorized to lean upon or trust in the arm of flesh? Were they ever enjoined by his precepts or example to mix in the policy of nations, or the councils of men? If not,—then let every one who desires to be found in his proper place, be on his guard, and beware of becoming connected in any of those departments where a humble dependence upon the Divine counsel is not prevalent, and where the policy of the world is permitted to supply the place of the doctrines of the gospel.

If there is any doctrine that is of greater value to mankind than another, it is the doctrine of *Divine revelation to man.* This is the fact, because this doctrine seems to support the opinion that it is a *living, discerning, and ever-active principle*, and is always present in the mind,—and has power in itself capable of keeping the mind sensible of its duty to God and also to man. Take away this active spiritual Monitor, and place our duties in a written form, and in that case we may attend to the obligations that are written, just when it happens to fit our inclination. Under such circumstances we may readily see that duties which may be admitted to be of the first importance, would be very often neglected. But, according to the views of Friends, those who believe in Divine revelation have a teacher within them by which they are ever kept sensible of the will of God ; and unless they wilfully rebel against the light that makes manifest their duties, they are walking in it, and therefore know that they are approved by it. These have the evidence of the Spirit itself bearing witness with their spirits, that they are the children of the Light and of the day.

The religion of these possessors is therefore not built upon a written dead testimony ; but is a religion that is always kept alive in the soul by the presence of the spirit of God. Now the professor of this religion knows daily whether he is in an acceptable state with his Lord and Master, or not. If he is, it is because he has entered into the Divine mind, and it is his comfort to feel a peaceful quiet. Such are not beating the air, nor are they in any doubt about themselves. They have Christ the true Light that lighteth every man that cometh into the world ; and being in and under his government, they are his subjects, and therefore know that they are members of his church and kingdom.

It is in this state that the saints of God can " rejoice evermore, and pray without ceasing." That is, they are always in that state which agrees with the Divine mind, and this is a state of prayer without ceasing : and hence also in everything they can give thanks. Now it is by this kind of spiritual and practical knowledge that the real followers of Christ become true Christians. They have entered into the New-covenant state, in which old things are done away, and all things become new, and all things of God. These are such Christians as cannot be satisfied with the mere externals of religion ; because, having a living knowledge of the immortal and eternal life, any thing short of this is but as the shadow without the substance.

Such is the religious experience of the faithful sons of God. It was the happy state of the apostles of Jesus Christ; and hence they could say, "We know that the son of God is come, and that he hath given us an understanding, that we may know him that is true, and we are in him that is true." Such is the religion of vital Christianity; and with these a knowledge of the will of God is ever present, and they need not that any man should teach them the knowledge of God, because the anointing which they have received abides with them, and is "Truth, and is no lie."

In viewing the present state of the Society of Friends, my mind has been deeply affected, and it appears to me that we are in danger of losing that state of unity and brotherly regard which once happily reigned in nearly all its departments. Some of the causes of this declension I shall endeavor to open for the consideration of others.

The Society of Friends has been made use of in the Divine hand, on the great subject of the enslaved Africans and their descendants. When this concern was first opened among Friends, it came from individual minds; and at that day many Friends held slaves. Hence it was found, that in attending to the subject, it was necessary that the condition of the master, as well as that of the slave, should receive proper consideration. Friends were therefore careful in all their labors, that the judgment of the claimant should be rightly informed upon the subject, as well as that the slave should obtain his freedom. Pursuing the concern with these feelings and views in relation to it, they were favored so to act, that an open door was kept with all; and therefore in the whole course of their labors for the redemption of the Society from the evil of slaveholding, the unity of the Society was preserved.

When through patient persevering labor, Friends had gained the important point of their own freedom from the evil, they were then prepared to hold up this subject to the notice of others. Being preserved in unity among themselves, this righteous testimony was held up with great care and judgment. It was not long before a law was obtained in Pennsylvania, declaring all colored persons born after the passing of the act, to be free after a stated period;—the males at twenty-eight years of age, if recorded within six months after birth, and the females at twenty-one years. But if not recorded within six months after birth, they were to be free, at twenty-one, the males, and the females at eighteen years. When this law was passed in Pennsylvania, it seemed like an entering wedge upon the subject; and it was followed by other laws that had an effect upon the great cause of freedom to the slave; and the important concern seemed to be gaining ground in the public mind.

In this state of the progress of this righteous testimony, it was seen that from emancipations which were taking place, and from various other causes, we were becoming surrounded by those people of color who were free by law. There were also some who would run away from servitude, and there were men who would take up others who were legally free, and claim them as slaves. It was from this state of things, that a protecting Society was formed in Philadelphia; the object of which was professedly to prevent kidnapping, and also to secure those colored people from being taken into bondage whose freedom took place, or was to take place by virtue of the law. For it was found that such as were born after the year 1780, and who would, even if recorded, be free at twenty-eight and twenty years, were liable to be sold by avaricious slaveholders into interminable bondage. These were among the objects of the care of this Abolition Society; and by their watchful care, the freedom of many were secured, who would otherwise have been sold in distant places into endless slavery.

This Society was composed of Friends and other active and intelligent men: and in their engagements to protect and assist the colored people, it sometimes happened that they would get hold of a case where the claim to the slave would be supported. Whenever this occurred, there would follow a liberal amount of reflections upon Friends. They would be accused of disregarding all law, if they could gain the freedom of the slave. This Association continued in operation for a number of years; and at length, from the falling off of many of the members who were not Friends,—the Society was held up among the Southern members of Congress, as being exclusively made up of members who belonged to the Society of Friends. This opinion was so fixed that a member of the Senate came out in that body with a mass of reflections upon Friends, built upon a case which he stated as one that was managed by Quakers. This circumstance gave an opportunity to correct the error, and to inform the public that those persons who had been engaged in it, were not in that case acting as Friends, but were members of an Association composed of persons of different religious professions; and therefore it was not fair to charge the proceedings of that body upon Friends.

As before stated, Friends have always on the subject of slavery, thought it right for them to keep an open door with the slaveholders. They have therefore in their movements on this subject endeavored to aim at letting them see that our object was their comfort and happiness,—that, being convinced in our experience of the great evil of the practice, it has become with us a religious concern, that our fellow citizens should get clear of it. But although we believe that it would be for the good of our country to see an end to all the evils of this system of great injustice and cruelty,—it appears to us to be a concern that nothing short of Divine wisdom can rightly dispose of. In all the movements of Friends, it has been their concern to know that they are not acting in their own will as men, but that they are guided by the all wise Head of the church. Now it is believed that it is under the leadings of this pure principle alone that the great cause of the enslaved Africans and their descendants can ever be conducted to a proper and correct issue; and believing also, as Friends have always done, that the masters are to be redeemed from the evils of slavery,—they have therefore uniformly had their minds turned to their situation, as well as to the operation of the system upon the slaves.

Hence, when we have been called to consider the subject, Friends have frequently avoided taking hold of it, because they did not see any course pointed out which would complete a general relief to both masters and slaves; and it has been left for further and more perfect openings to turn up in favor of their taking hold of the important subject. Under those circumstances, many of our members have believed that the concern has been left without the attention being given to it, which the suffering condition of those held in slavery calls for. Such individuals, supposing that they have seen something that could be done, have gone into activity in the business, and are blaming the society for having failed to come forward, and take hold with them and pursue the subject in their way. But as Friends do not see their way, the subject must be left.

In this state of things there has appeared to be danger of the unity and harmony of the society being much injured, and more or less of a division formed therein. Friends must, notwithstanding, abide by and in their own principles,—the principles of Truth. They stand as a society upon very important ground. To them is committed the momentous testimony of professing a practical belief in a divine gift to man; and they are bound in agreement with this profession, to stand opposed to every religious pretension, where the individuals can proceed to act without the pure and blessed testimony of this Divine gift. They are also bound by the solemnity of their profession, to reject, as contrary to the benign purposes of the Christian's duty, all movements under the character of religion, which are made in the will and wisdom of man. It being in their view, contrary to the great principles laid down by Christ and his apostles, for any step to be taken with a view to advance the cause of universal righteousness, that is not dictated by the immediate openings and leadings of the spirit of Christ.

Now as Friends are apparently the only people who

make this profession, they are in duty bound carefully to maintain this important ground. To preserve the society in agreement with this high profession, it appears very important that they should avoid mixing with others; and that they should abide in a state of faithful attention to their religious principles. By so doing, and conforming in practice to the clear openings of our religious testimonies, we shall fulfill all that is required at our hands; and Friends may thus expect to be preserved in unity one with another, and with the great and glorious Head of the Church. As the society keeps on this ground, it will be favored with the necessary qualifications to perform the duties unto which it has been, or may be called. The work of our redemption and salvation is a work that can never be carried on by our own powers alone. It must be performed by the aid of the gift of God; and therefore we must learn to understand its testimonies, before we can be numbered among the true followers of Christ. It appears to me therefore, that if Friends continue to be useful in the cause of righteousness, *we must stand alone*, and be faithful to the precious gift which we have received from our gracious Helper. If at any time we suffer our minds to wander from the proper abiding place, we may expect to be caught and carried away into something that it would be better for us to keep clear of. Oh! the concern and travail of my spirit, that the society of Friends may be preserved in its proper place, and answer the great end, for which I am persuaded it was raised up.

ON THE ORDER AND DISCIPLINE OF SOCIETY.

To understand the foundation and nature of the Discipline of Friends, it is necessary that we should take into view the government of the church in what may be called its more civil concerns. Among the apostles and primitive believers, it was found to be needful for the comfort and harmony of their society to adopt conclusions and regulations for the government and observance of the members in their more outward walking and conduct toward one another.

Hence at an early period we find that the body of the apostles and elders met at Jerusalem to deliberate upon, and determine what regulations should be made for the government of the social conduct of such Gentile converts as were added to the church. For this circumstance occasioned a diversity of opinion among the Jewish believers. Now it may be reasonably believed that when the church was met at Jerusalem for considering the important subject, that each member opened his views of the proper order to be observed, and that those opinions would be likely to be diverse and various at first. Such we find to have been the fact in that meeting. But we also find that after these various opinions and disputings on the question at issue, all the multitude were brought into a state of silence, listening to the views held up by Barnabas and Paul. After they had fully opened the case, an elder rose up and was the instrument of setting the subject of discipline before them, so that they all united in the conclusion, that it seemed good to the Holy Spirit and to the church to prescribe only a few necessary things as rules of discipline in the case.

The discipline of the society of Friends had a similar origin. It arose from the necessity of cases that required the united conclusion of the body in order to preserve the harmony of the members. Thus, rules and regulations have been made from time to time, adapted to the circumstances and necessities of the Society. It is therefore obvious that the order and discipline of Friends from the beginning to the present time, have been established in the general unity of the body. If any member is not satisfied with any particular rule of discipline or custom of the society, he has the right and privilege of opening it in his own Monthly Meeting for consideration; and if his brethren unite with his objections, the case is next to be brought before a Quarterly Meeting; and thence, if approved, it goes to the Yearly Meeting. But if that meeting should not believe that it is necessary to make a change, it becomes the duty of the member who was dissatisfied, and all others, to submit to the conclusion of the body. But should he, or any other member refuse to submit to the judgment of the Yearly Meeting, such individuals should be no longer considered as sound members; because they stand opposed to the united judgment of their brethren in a case where every privilege has been allowed them, that is consistent with the existence and well-being of society.

Now we have cause to regret, that notwithstanding the liberality of our system, and the evidence we have that the harmony of society cannot be maintained, but by submitting to the judgment of the body,—there are those who publicly oppose the conclusions that have been agreed to by the Yearly Meeting. Of this class are some who have been approved as ministers and active members, and who continue to be appointed by Monthly Meetings to services in the society. Now this subject appears to require deeper consideration; for if a member who manifestly does not unite with the order and discipline of the society, should be appointed on a committee to deal with another member as an offender for a breach of order or discipline, it would be obviously inconsistent, and must tend to weakness.

From the first rise of the society it has been the practice of Friends to rise and uncover the head in the time of vocal prayer. Some difference of sentiment having occurred, this subject was brought before our Yearly Meeting not many years ago, and on deliberate consideration Friends did not approve of declining the practice. Now, as no member can reasonably expect the whole body of the Society to submit to his opinion, there appears no other way for the society to remain united but for those who think differently from their friends patiently to bear their own burdens, and conform to the sense of the body: and if they would condescend to do so, and have the truth on their side, it may confidently be believed that in due time the way will open for their views to obtain. But should any persist in a course of conduct manifesting their disunity with the order of society, and in opposition thereto—such showing a want of condescension, give proof to their Friends that it would be dangerous to themselves, as well as prejudicial to the society, to countenance them in their present state of mind. For, notwithstanding such may allege that their deviation from the custom of rising in time of vocal prayer, is not from any opposition or dislike to the person appearing, yet it tends to produce disunity and confusion. And even those who plead a conscientious scruple in the case, would act a more honorable part if they were to withdraw from the society.

LETTER TO HIS SON, JOSEPH.

After parting on second day we rode home, and found Jesse about as he had been for some time past, and to all appearance not gaining any strength. His complaint of the bowels appears to be the main difficulty, and is no doubt a consequence resulting from a general state of his system. We do not yet despair of his recovery,—although we think there is not much for our hopes to rest upon. We both felt sorry on coming away that we had not seen William, and had some conversation with him. If nothing offers better for him in the spring, I shall find him employment here upon some plan that may answer.

In thy case we have had our tender feelings much awakened. To think of a son with a family looking up to him for what they stand in need of, and to know that it is not in his power to do anything for them, nor even for himself,—is a circumstance which has made a deep impression with us. And it has been increased by the fact, that it is not in our power to afford the assistance which it would be our pleasure to do. But though such is the state of the case we cannot be too thankful to find that thy mind has been supported through all, and kept in a happy state of resignation. By keeping in this state, it will give to thy constitution every advantage in favor of recovering health; and no doubt, though no way may at present be seen to get along, yet something will sooner or later turn up that will be found to answer. If however, thy time should be but short in this world, and all these concerns come to an end, I am not without faith that all may wind up for the best, both to thee and thine. For myself, I find ample cause to believe, that though many and great changes have occurred with me, it is out of the power of all the world to take away my confidence in the care and blessing of that special Providence which has been my joy and comfort when all others have failed.

The world and its opinions and interests, I am convinced are too highly valued by many. But the fact is, that those who have been the most useful in it, and have enjoyed the greatest share of real independence and happiness, have been men and women who have never set their hearts upon it, and who have wisely submitted themselves to the course of events in the firm faith, that having done what they could, nothing more was required. It is far from my desire to produce any improper feeling in the mind, either on thy own account or mine. I am now principally concerned that thou may turn away all unnecessary anxiety about either thyself or us, and that we may mutually take things as they occur and be satisfied.

Those medical men with whom I have spoken say that there is more hope of a case where bleeding of the lungs has been produced by exertion, than there is when it comes on without any previous excitement. With sincere love, in which thy mother unites, I remain thy father,

Jesse Kersey.

He who was famed for wisdom at one period of his life said, "A man that hath friends, must show himself friendly; and there is a friend that sticketh closer than a brother."

By this friend I understand king Solomon to mean the Divine gift, or the manifestation of the spirit of God. To know the teaching of this gift, and clearly to distinguish it from the impressions made upon the mind by other causes, has been supposed to be almost impossible. But our difficulty in the case does not arise from any mysterious circumstance connected with the subject;—but from the habitual tendency in the minds of many of looking for more than is consistent with the wisdom of God to grant or furnish. We should be content with such indications of the Divine voice as are to be heard in the soul, when we are gathered into a state of separation from all worldly ideas or images of material things. When the mind may be said to be alone, and centered in a state of inward stillness; it is then that God speaks to man, when he is in a waiting state, and has not any other thing to occupy his attention. Under this circumstance, it pleases him to manifest himself to his creatures. If it be to rebuke us for any mistake we have made, or to reprove us for any improper action or conduct we have been guilty of,—we feel the rebuke by the sense of condemnation spread over us. If no rebuke has been merited, we may feel a humbling and tender impression of his love, by the calming influence of which we may be satisfied that we are favored with a feeling sense of the goodness of God towards us.

With a view, however, more fully to illustrate the important doctrine of the teaching of this divine gift, it may be remarked that we find it confirmed by all the penmen of the holy scriptures. The word of the Lord was communicated to Noah, and he in obedience thereto built the ark. It appeared to Abraham; and he was thus informed of the intended destruction of Sodom and Gomorrah. From those two eminent men I might go on to name all the great characters found in the Old Testament; and to these might be added all the apostles mentioned in the New, for they all agree in testimony to the manifestation of the spirit to the mind of Man. It is therefore an extraordinary case, that any who profess a belief in the scriptures of Truth, should doubt the reality of this precious gift of God to man.

THE religious society of Friends have known what it was to feel the weight of persecution; and history furnishes ample proof that a great part of the suffering which Friends have had to pass through, has been at the instance of the Priests. Finding at length that it was impossible to force Friends to desert the ground which they believed they were called to stand upon in supporting the testimonies of Truth,—this same class of men have of latter time resorted to other means to accomplish their purpose. They have turned their attention to some of the testimonies of Truth embraced and professed by Friends, and would seem to want to promote the same. They have therefore formed associations in order to accomplish their purpose of drawing Friends away from their original ground, and getting them to join with others in advancing these righteous testimonies by means of popular opinion, and the excitement of the passions and sympathies of the natural man. For this purpose they instituted Peace Societies,—Temperance Societies,—Abolition, or Anti-Slavery Societies,—and many others.

Now the priests themselves have not in person appeared as the most active agents in the formation of these associations, and the publication of newspapers, pamphlets, &c. But it is somewhat singular that their lecturers should come into the neighborhoods of Friends, and deliver their lectures and take other measures among them, in aid of their cause. But here appears to be the object to get our members to join in these associations, and so break the unity of the society. For, when they find there are many Friends who do not think it right to form any alliances with them and their measures and manners,—but on the contrary, in agreement with our religious principles and persuasion, believe it obligatory for the society to maintain its original ground of waiting for the mind of Truth to qualify them for rightly moving in support of its testimonies,—those lecturers and some of our fellow professors who join with them, take the liberty to call in question the integrity of their brethren and fellow members,—and charge them with having lessened in their concern and testimony on those subjects, and become lukewarm and indifferent.

Now, for the sake of preserving, if possible such of our members as so join with the agents of priestcraft, and doubt the faithfulness and uprightness of their brethren, it seems necessary to remind them of the difference which has always existed between Friends and others. As a religious society, we profess to believe that it is not in the power of man to promote or advance the Lord's work by the mere efforts of his own will and contrivance. But we have ever believed that every step in the support and advancement of the testimonies of truth, must be taken in conformity with the clear openings of the Light of Truth itself. Now, as we cannot command this Light or its openings at any time we may please, we have always professed to wait for its blessed shining in us, to direct us and qualify us for service. Hence we cannot mingle in association with those who are always ready, and who do not profess to believe in such openings of the mind of Truth,—but rely upon the reason and talents of the natural man, and the activity of his creaturely powers.

THERE is no subject which has engaged the pens of theological writers that appears to be less understood than that of the origin of evil. It is probable that one great reason why this continues to be the case is because it has been customary to begin the enquiry in the wrong place. If instead of going to the time of Adam we were to begin with ourselves it is probable we should become more acquainted with the nature of the subject and with the inlets and causes of it. But before it is possible to unfold this important concern clearly we shall find that it is necessary to examine what it is that constitutes evil—on this point there may be a variety of opinions and hence one of the difficulties which we have to encounter, and which we shall try to remove by taking into view what may be admitted as the perfect and what the imperfect state of man. And first as to the perfect state, admitting as we are bound to do, that God is a spirit and consequently a being of unlimited intelligence, it seems reasonable to believe that in the perfect state of man he must be united to his Creator, and that to maintain the standing of a perfect man this state of complete union must be kept to. While then the spirit of man is kept in perfect union with his glorious original there can be no such thing as sin or evil. This view of the subject is supported by the testimony of the scriptures. They inform us that as many as are led by the spirit of God they are the sons of God. Hence we see that to be led by the Divine Spirit is to follow a guide that keeps us free from evil, and therefore had the human race lived under this government there would have been no such thing as moral evil in the world. On the contrary as all would be in the way of the leadings of this Heavenly Guide, all would be preserved on the ground of innocence and in complete union with a blessed Creator. We are consequently to understand that evil commenced with the first act of disobedience to the duty enjoined by the Divine Spirit and this is what produces evil in every one that becomes a sinner. So long then as man is faithful to the manifestations of the Spirit of God, he is free from sin and has this spirit bearing witness with his spirit that he is a son and heir of the heavenly kingdom. To such a subject there is no condemnation. Because agreeably to the testimony of the apostle Paul these find that there is no condemnation to them which are in Christ Jesus who walk not after the flesh but after the spirit. It follows from this view that the sins of mankind are produced by disobedience to the spirit or by yielding to the desires of our animal or fleshy nature. If this be the fact we are no longer at a loss to determine what it is that constitutes evil, but we see clearly that it is a consequence that arises from animal indulgences entered into in opposition to the immediate impression of the Divine Spirit. Having in a concise manner shown that a sinful state is that in which the will of man is opposed to the Divine will. We are now to examine into the causes that have an influence over the will. It is found to be acted upon by various objects, and these are presented to it through the outward senses. Almost all the operations of those senses are involuntary—and therefore it is not in the power of man to prevent the presentation of objects which may tempt him and draw him off from the way in which he should go. Now as those presentations are involuntary it depends upon the uprightness of the will to the leadings of the Divine Spirit whether it will reject those temptations involuntarily introduced or embrace them. In case it should decide upon the latter there is then a state of evil introduced. Hence we may see that from the freedom of the will a door was opened for good or evil.

In the preservation of the society upon Christian ground there is perhaps no subject of greater importance than that of the ministry. If this should become lifeless and formal the meetings of Friends would then cease to be edifying or instructive. It is therefore a subject that should be watched with godly care and jealousy. Friends have thought it right in order to have a ministry that should agree in character and kind with that of the apostles' days that when any appear as Ministers they should be held for a time on trial and after they had appeared in that line for some time, to recommend them to the Quarterly Meeting of Ministers and Elders. If that meeting should believe that the individual has received a gift and is called to the service they record his name as one that they have approved, but if the Quarterly Meeting of Ministers and Elders do not unite, in that case the individual is not owned by the society as a minister. If he is owned as a minister he is then considered by his friends as one called to the solemn service, and it is the duty of the elders to watch over him, and as they see occasion, to caution and warn him against all errors, either by saying too much or too little, or in any other manner acting contrary to the openings and pure leadings of the gift. There is no concern in which the society should be more upon its guard than that of the ministry. When those who believe that they are called to this service depart from the precious life and become active in the mere will of the creature,—if such are permitted to go on they soon furnish occasion for painful exercise to their brethren, and if they are suffered to continue are apt to become very obstinate in their opinion, and sometimes will suffer themselves to be disowned by their friends rather than submit to be advised, or in any manner regulated in their movements.

It has often been cause of deep concern where persons become self-willed and not disposed to regard any opinion but their own. Such have run out from less to more until there was no room or place in their minds for advice. It has often been matter of wonder why any should so far presume upon their own judgment as obstinately to oppose their best friends on this subject, when it must be clear that when the communications of an individual are objected to by the meeting where they are offered they can be of no use. There are, no doubt, individuals furnished with a clear view of the nature of gospel ministry, in order that they might be proper judges of the ministry in the society, and this may be a purpose of divine wisdom in furnishing such a sight and judgment. It is obviously a matter of great importance to come to a right judgment on the subject. We may therefore conclude that it is acting the part of wisdom for such as Friends cannot approve, to submit to the judgment of their brethren rather than to go in their own self-will and wound the feelings of such as are concerned for their welfare. It is a mark of weak judgment, when those who know that their communications are not satisfactory continue to impose them upon the society. Because if they would consider the effect, they must be convinced that all their engagements in that line were to their own prejudice and the injury of the cause. Sometimes Friends may become prejudiced against the testimony of an individual improperly and be the means of involving an honest mind in very serious trial that might have been avoided if there had been the exercise of more patience. But let the motive or reason have been what it may. If a person after appearing in the ministry finds that the way is not open, no better course can be taken than that of bearing their own burden for a time. Thus the meeting will eventually see and be satisfied that the testimonies are offered as a positive duty and that there is no self-will or stubbornness in the case. There is a precious simplicity and dignity in all those communications that are the fruit of the Divine Spirit that can never be imitated by the art of man. It is therefore much to be desired that all who believe they are called to this solemn and weighty concern might carefully wait for the openings and leadings of the true Spirit of the Gospel in their concerns to speak among the people. It is not only necessary to know the puttings forth of the great Head of the Church but we should also know when we are engaged in speaking to the people how to divide the word in such manner as to produce the right effect upon the minds of the hearers. There is a right time to close a testimony as well as a right time to commence it, and where a Friend remains too long on his feet and the service begins to fail to command the true and solemnizing effect, it is much better to stop short and sit down than to continue, without the life and power is felt to be in dominion. These are considerations connected with the ministry that may seem of minor importance but nevertheless deserve to be attended to by all those who feel bound to the work. In the wisdom of the great Head of the Church we discover that he has bestowed upon our organic nature powers of utterance and hence it is that we have the capacity of understanding one another. The powers of communication by speech are very valuable, and in the occupancy of these powers we may become so well accomplished as to be easily and well understood. We may also acquire habits that would make it difficult for another to understand anything that we say. On this part of the concern it appears that in the primitive church the apostles recommended to hold fast the form of sound words. Now by this we may understand that they had a respect to the use of such terms as might be understood. And it would seem that they also must have had a respect to the manner of delivery as well as to the matter delivered. It has frequently been observed that those in the ministry amongst Friends fail to employ their own natural voices and often fall into the habit of making use of an unnatural one, and are therefore sometimes not easily understood. Now although this may be considered as the less important part of the concern it is nevertheless entitled to some consideration. Those who adopt a clear and intelligent manner of speaking are generally acceptable among their friends.

20th of 2d month, 1841.

In the origin of religious society it is reasonable to suspect that there should be a cause or a motive to justify a new establishment, and where such cause or motive is well founded the society may be considered as coming forth on a justifiable ground. To form sects or parties merely out of respect to a popular individual has more the appearance of an evil than a good in it. There has been at different periods of the world such a state of religious sentiment and such conditions of society as have no doubt furnished just occasion for dissention and for becoming organized under a different name and with different views. Such was the fact when Martin Luther dissented from the Romish church. It was impossible for him to prevail upon that church to give up the doctrine of a purgatory or the faith it entertained in the Host and various other particulars which might be mentioned. It remained therefore for him to establish a separate society. Luther was acting in agreement with his judgment when he opposed the superstition of the Romish Church. In his labors to improve the profession of religion all that he could do was to enlighten others as far as he had been enlightened himself. His establishment though separated from many of the useless forms of those that preceded him was not perfect or at least it embraced for its government forms and duties which subsequent reformers have deemed incompatible with the spirituality of the gospel. From this cause the way remained open for the gathering new societies. But when in the progress of the light of the gospel individuals were raised up who banished all unnecessary formalities and had embraced and cultivated the true Christian doctrines a foundation was gained incapable of reform. All subsequent divisions of Christian professors into sects and parties seem to have risen out of motives that are doubtful, and there is reason to doubt the soundness of their origin. Especially if it be true that the only justifiable cause for forming a new sect is that of arriving at a perfect society and a correct profession of Christian doctrine. There is, however, reason to believe that there have been many sects established upon the mere preference given to a popular preacher. If establishments upon such motives are to obtain credit we shall look in vain for stability in the Christian world. One will continue to say I am of Paul, another, I am of Apollos, and I of Cephas. But upon such preferences it was never designed that religious communities should be formed; because were such a foundation countenanced or admitted it would open the way for every ambitious preacher to become the head of a party, and by this means the name of Christianity would be brought into contempt. So far therefore as the professors of the name of Christ have been divided from one another by following men rather than principles of faith,to the same extent the cause of universal righteousness has been injured. To restore the church of Christ to harmony and to produce that oneness which was in the beginning must be the ardent desire of every true disciple. Or in other words to produce unanimity among the professors of religion; for as to the living members of the church they must at all times be as the multitude of the believers were in the beginning, " of one heart and of one soul," because the same mind that was in Christ is always to live in his followers and as this is experienced it takes away all division and they are one, even as He and the Father are one. With a view to bring about this oneness the present essay has been attempted. It has been clear to the writer that the divided state of mankind on the great subject of the soul's redemption is not a consequence of true religion but that it must be owing to a want of it. Whatever causes have contributed to produce this state of things, or remain in support of the divided state of the professors of religion he believes when all agree to lay down every degree of sectarian pride and prejudice, union of mind and judgment will follow; and the sincere disciples of Christ finding that they are all possessed of the same mind that they are governed by the same spirit that dwelt in Christ, and knowing that if any man have not the spirit of Christ he is none of his. They will necessarily be one even as He and his Father are one. To promote this great and blessed union that might extend from sea to sea and from the rivers to the ends of the earth must be to advance an object of the greatest value to mankind. Why then are we divided as at present? Is the religion of Jesus Christ who came to put an end to sin to finish transgression and in the room thereof to bring in everlasting righteousness of such a mysterious and hidden nature that its duties are not to be comprehended. How then did the Prophet Isaiah fall into so great a mistake as to say that the wayfaring man though a fool shall not err therein. Let all men think for themselves and examine what tends to produce in their own minds the greatest confidence, the most perfect peace and happiness, and when they find this they will find the same thing in which the multitude of believers were united in the beginning. They will find that light that makes manifest all the unfruitful works of darkness a light which according to St. John enlightens every man that comes into the world. The same that gives man to see the error of his way and convinces the understanding of what there is occasion to repent of, what must be forsaken and given up in order to have fellowship with it. In this state it will be easy to see that the object of our devotion is the same. That the church of Christ has always been composed of members in unity one with another and that however religious professors may divide from one another. This church is made up of those that live in the light and walk in the light even as he is in the light and therefore they necessarily have fellowship with each other. It was this same light which the apostle Paul calls the spirit, a measure whereof is given to every man to profit withal. The Spirit of Truth: the same which the blessed Jesus promised to his disciples and which was to teach them all things and bring all things to their remembrance. Accordingly we find his promise fulfilled to them on the memorable day of Pentecost,—when the Holy Ghost was sent down from heaven and rested on each of them, concerning which the apostle Peter bore testimony to the multitude and informed them. "This is that which was spoken by the Prophet Joel saying, it shall come to pass in the latter days that I will pour forth of my spirit upon all flesh and your sons and your daughters shall prophesy &c." To this gift of the spirit this light to enlighten the Gentiles, and for God's salvation to the ends of the earth the Holy Sciptures give ample testimony. In the early state of the Christian Church the Holy Spirit was received, believed in and obeyed. It was in their estimation, Christ within, the hope of Glory, the Power of God, and the Wisdom of God the same that was in the beginning of his creation and by which the worlds were made, the Alpha and the Omega. By the manifestation whereof the Gospel was preached in every creature. To which angels, principalities and powers, things in Heaven and in earth were to be subject. Under the immediate teaching whereof the Holy Scriptures were written. While the members considered this heavenly gift paramount to all other guides or means of Faith they were a united body and their preaching and their example had a powerful influence upon mankind, and the reason was this that they that heard them had the witness in themselves. But when the testimonies of those who were witnesses of the spirit were received by subsequent believers and held in preference to the spirit itself, then disagreement followed; one class urging one thing, and another urging another, one saying I am of Paul and another I am of Apollos, &c. Some contending for circumcision, some for a respect to the Jewish restrictions upon the articles of food and others for regarding one day above another; others again esteeming every day alike. By such division and excuses of division the professors in process of time were separated and different doctrines obtained credit. Hence a door was opened for controversy and for the exercise of the wisdom, will and talents of men to take the lead in ordering and managing the plain simple concerns of the Church. Under these circumstances the fathers of one period were found at variance with those of another and contradictory systems and opinions obtained credit and were supported by their several parties and friends and that which in its rise gave the occasion of division, though it was viewed no doubt by the sincere followers as an occasion of regret and as likely to produce weakness and disorder, in the end became at length common, and apparently as at this day without remedy. Thus we may easily find the origin of the multiplicity of sects and parties among the professors of the name of Christ. While the sincere mind is taking a view of this progressive decline in the standing and character of the professed friends of Christianity, it is impossible not to deplore the melancholy change, and the same spirit which leads to mourn over the many divisions and parties which now exists will necessarily lead to the desire that they should become again united. If we believe that the doctrines of Christianity are plain and simple, and that which it is necessary for a man to believe in order to be a Christian may be readily attained, may we not conclude that a union might be perfected and a restoration gained to the primitive standing of the followers of Christ. To accomplish this great object it appears to the author there is but one way, and that is to go back to the ground from whence we have departed. If we do so we shall not depend on the externals of religion, but come under the guidance of the same spirit as believed in in the beginning. We shall admit of the same liberties in obedience to this spirit which obtained among the prophets and apostles. Those liberties were not calculated to weaken the ties of moral obligation or in any degree to separate man from his fellow man. Our first enquiry with a view to return to the primitive state of the Church will be made into the duties which were deemed of positive obligation: these we shall attempt to separate from those of less weight and importance—and first as to ministers. Those of this class or character were to be gifted by the Divine spirit for the service. It was not thought possible that a man would be made a minister by any human means. This qualification was purely the gift of the Spirit, and a woe rested upon such if they did not preach the gospel. Paul informs us that the gospel which he preached he received not from man neither was he taught but by the revelation of Jesus Christ.

And for this cause the Most High made choice of him to make of him both a minister and a witness, delivering him from the people and from the Gentiles "to whom now I send thee to open their eyes and to turn them from darkness to light and from the power of Satan unto God that they might receive forgiveness of their sins" and thus be united to the church of Christ. This apostle having freely received thought it was his duty freely to give, laboring with his own hands that he might not make the gospel chargeable to any. He did not preach by contracts or attempt after this manner to abuse his power in the gospel—nor did he ever alledge that his qualifications for the ministry were gained by outward or literary means. The same is the fact in relation to all his companions in the work both male and female. They were all spiritually called and all bound by him that called them freely to minister what they had freely received. It may be remarked too that they did not believe the gospel stood in word only, but in power. Of this they gave ample testimony, and appear clearly to demonstrate that in their opinion the Gospel of Jesus Christ was the Power of God unto Salvation to all them that believe. To men and women who had this kind of understanding of the ministry of the gospel nothing could appear more preposterous than an attempt to sell it for money; I say to men and women because that women took part in the ministry is evident as acknowledged by the testimony of the Holy Scriptures. On this subject there has been among the professors of Christianity a melancholy change. They who now claim the character of ministers seem to think that they are entitled to it because they have acquired a knowledge of the Oriental Languages ; they understand the Greek and the Hebrew and are therefore prepared in their own estimation to stand in the solemn office of ministers. But although those attainments may be supposed to have their advantages in a literary point of view, it is impossible that they should prepare any to turn a dark and deluded world from darkness to Light and from the power of Satan unto God. Of course they cannot prepare an individual to fulfill the important work of the ministry from all which we may surely believe that the numerous theological seminaries instead of producing union among the professors of Christianity will be instrumental in separating them if possible still wider one from another. Those schools will receive for ministerial education young persons who when they complete their studies will take it for granted that they must be clothed with the title of Doctors in Divinity—at the same time the truly enlightened Christian will think of them very differently—because such must always believe that it is not for man to select the officers in the church of Christ, any more than it is for him to furnish the requisite gifts or talents. Hence the Divines of human ordination will always be estimated as having taken the presumed ground of worldly wisdom : in consequence of which it will be impossible for them to be the instruments of union in the church of Christ.

PERHAPS there is no disposition common to man, which has been the cause of more strife and confusion than the love of power and preference. We have an example of this kind given in the case of the mother of Zebedee's children who came to Jesus, worshipping him, and soliciting for her two sons that they might be preferred by him when he should come into his kingdom. But it may be easily perceived that he disapproved of the application, and adopted a plan which should serve to convince his followers that this was a state of mind which they were not to countenance. He reminded them how it was among the Gentiles. "The princes," says he, "of the Gentiles exercise dominion over them; but it shall not be so among you, but whosoever will be great among you let him be your minister. And whosoever will be chief among you let him be your servant. Even as the Son of Man came not to be ministered unto but to minister, and to give his life a ransom for many." If in religious society the doctrine given in the foregoing case had been wisely regarded, much evil might have been prevented. The Society of Friends, once a happy people, and in many respects an example to others, might have remained in perfect harmony, had they maintained that humility of mind and manners, so continually required by the Great and Holy Head. But a spirit opposed to the meekness and gentleness of the dear Son of God, having obtained the dominion over us, it was impossible for us in this state to maintain anything like unity. Nor will any society long remain united while those turbulent tempters are permitted to rule. To gain the Lamb's victory we must always expect it through patient suffering. All conquests sought in any other way, must be connected with that spirit which obtains its end by confused noises and garments rolled in blood. Hence it is said that "cursed is the man that trusteth in man, and maketh flesh his arm." With carnal weapons the Christian can take no part. He is to come himself, body, soul and spirit, under the yoke of Christ; and in this state he has entered into the Kingdom of Righteousness, peace, and joy in the Holy Spirit.

Now it cannot be that any of these living members, while they are under and subject to the precious Gift, will ever desire to bear rule over the minds and consciences of their brethren. And if such at any time should feel in themselves a spirit of domination, they would know that in it there could be no peace. It is not the design of our Holy Head, if we may judge either from his example, or his precepts, that the members of his church should ever depend upon the arm of flesh for its government; and therefore it is the duty of his members to employ no other power for the conquest of disorders, than the power of Love. When this does not succeed, the living must take their stand in the everlasting patience. It has been the portion of the faithful to have trials. They have seen unruly spirits and they have suffered from them the loss of everything, and even life itself, but this was their victory, even their faith, which they held in a pure conscience; and to such all things have worked together for good. They have found that all manner of evil spirits were made subject to them in the Lord's time; and as they have placed all their hope and confidence in him, so they have not been suffered to fall; but have stood firm and faithful to the end, and it is the end which crowns all.

Confiding in the truth of the foregoing doctrine,

and having the most powerful assurance that the gospel of Christ, which is the power of God unto salvation to all them that believe, consists of Love,—we are next to show that this is the state to which every follower of the Lamb of God is called. "A new commandment I give unto you, that ye love one another: even as I have loved you;" and "what greater love hath any man than this, that he lay down his life for his friend." Such are the precepts and such also was the example of the Saviour of men. He has condescended to be our instructor, and all those who become his subjects find that it is by living in love that they are preserved in the unity of the one eternal Spirit. As therefore pure and unfeigned love is to be the governing principle among Christians; it is evident that they can never depart from it and remain members of the church of Christ. When any therefore suffer their minds to be carried away from the mark of Discipleship, they cease to be Christians, and join themselves in spirit to a different order of men. As well might it be expected to make darkness light, or falsehood truth, as that any should depart from the Spirit of Love and at the same time be Christians; or, which is the same thing, disciples of Christ. But when this heavenly command to love one another is lived in, the members have passed from Darkness to Light, from the kingdom and government of this world, to the kingdom and government of the Prince of Peace. The great duty therefore of all the members of this heavenly kingdom is to keep clear of all strife and contention —to live in Love and keep it alive in the Lord, both towards God and man. Thus they will be without any defilement having their lamps trimmed and their lights burning.

In order to promote the gathering and perfect establishment of this true church of God, it is necessary that there should be raised up men and women of honest and sincere minds, who will not seek to obtain dominion over their brethren, nor suffer themselves to be carried away by any worldly object; but, believing in the great truths of the gospel, they will be careful to keep unspotted from the world. Not pleading for the indulgence of human infirmities, but walking in the light as He their Holy Head is light, they will have fellowship one with another. Oh the depth, both of the mercy and goodness of God, to such gathered souls! They have the power and the privilege given them to enter within the vail, and know what it is to witness the living power and presence of their holy teacher; who opens to them a sight and a sense of the Holy of Holies, where they can adore him that was, and is, and is to them to come in his own glory. The Lord of Hosts, the God of the spirits of all flesh is their Alpha and Omega. And because of the brightness of his coming, and the glory of his being, they can say that he is to them more than the increase of corn, wine, or oil. When these sons and daughters of the Most High are permitted to worship Him in the beauty of holiness, the shadows flee away; and they see that they are not now come to the mount that might not be touched; but on the contrary they have come "to Mount Sion, and unto the city of the living God, the heavenly Jerusalem, and to an innumerable company of angels, to the general assembly and church of the first-born which are written in heaven, and to God the judge of all, and to the spirits of just men made perfect." Such then are the living members of God's invisible church. Now this heavenly company can never be divided, but must be and remain the one eternal body of which Christ Jesus is the Head. And as the head is perfect, so must the body be perfect also; being fitly compacted and joined together by unlimited power and wisdom; and all the members of this living and heavenly body must be capable of a spiritual communion.

FAMILY EDUCATION.

We are now to look into the duties which are required, and must be fulfilled on the part of those sons and daughters of God. As they have entered into covenant with the Holy One of Israel, they are bound by pure love watchfully to regard all that is required of them to do: among the first and most solemn of obligations, the duty of commanding their households and those after them, can never be neglected without incurring the divine displeasure. It appears to have been a cause why the Almighty declared he would not hide from Abraham what he had determined to do with the people of Sodom and Gomorrah. "Shall I hide from Abraham the thing that I do, seeing that I know him, that he will command his children and his household, and they shall keep the way of the Lord?"

It is much to be lamented that many children are permitted to grow up in the Society of Friends, without their being ever taught the lesson of obedience to parents. The consequence is, that they in a state of manhood prove self-willed, if not stubborn ; nor have they scarcely any respect for the judgment of their parents, but live in opposition to the advice of their friends ; nor is it likely that such will ever make useful and agreeable members of society ; because being always indulged with their own gratifications, and never condescending to proper restraint they acquire a habit of obstinacy that ever after renders them disagreeable in all company. But children that are rightly educated are mild and pleasant in their disposition and manners. On this important concern much might be said ; but though it is of great consequence to the cause of Truth, it must under present circumstances be left ; not without sincere desire, however that it may obtain the serious attention of Friends. As it regards the schooling of the families of Friends, I have long doubted the fitness of large boarding institutions for this purpose. It appears to me that a child to be brought up properly, should never be separated from a connection with the domestic duties. If this was regarded according to the merits of it, parents would undergo many inconveniences rather than send their children from home to be educated. In my opinion the proper place for children to receive learning is in the house of the parent ; and this could be readily accomplished by a little attention to the proper occupancy of the time. In the winter farmers have the long evenings at leisure, and if the plan was adopted of bringing the books on the table after supper, two hours might be devoted to instruction every evening, and it would not be long before the father and the children would find it a very happy method of acquiring the necessary learning: they would ever be delighted with those pleasant modes of family improvement so that in many families the parents in a few years would see that their elder children were capable of supplying their places.

ON THE IMPORTANCE OF KEEPING UP OUR MEETINGS OF WORSHIP.

In reflecting upon the past and present condition of the society of Friends, and comparing the former with the latter there is much to indicate that Friends are on the decline. Formerly there was a great amount of love among them, and therefore it was their comfort and delight often to see one another: hence we find that religious meetings were carefully attended, and if at any time one of them was absent enquiry was made into the cause. By this means if any one was found to have neglected his or her duty the case was at once understood, and the individual received such help as was required and the society were prepared to help one another. But in proportion as the society fell away from this state they came into the condition of the Ephesian church, having left their first love. Thus the lively impressions and feeling of tender regard gradually declining there was not that care for one another that existed in the beginning, and members might be frequently absent from their religious meetings and none would feel sufficient concern to speak to him or her on the occasion. In this view of the decline of society it appears that in the first place a deficiency of a two-fold character gradually gained ground until we now have abundant cause to mourn over the present state of things at large amongst us. But our mourning and complaining will do but little for us. It is time for measures to be taken that may have some proper effect. In the first place it seems clear that we cannot kindle up again that ardent love of God and of one another that existed during the time of suffering under persecution. In that state of things there was much to awaken tender sympathy and engage Friends in considering the situation of the members and to administer relief. Those acts of kindness had a tendency to keep alive feelings of mutual regard, and hence we see that a change of situation has very much contributed to produce a change of character in the society. Since the spirit of persecution has subsided, Friends, as a body, have gone on in the pursuit of worldly concerns and being restrained by principle from indulging in the common extravagances of mankind they soon began to increase in the treasures of the world and thus as the occasions of suffering were removed the opportunities of seeing one another were not so frequent. By those changes in situation a change in habits and manners followed, and prosperity in their worldly pursuits has gradually introduced a selfish spirit; a spirit in its whole character differing from the generous and benign spirit of the gospel. In this way we may have the gradual but positive decline of many amongst us from that religious feeling which had so eminently attended the minds of Friends in the beginning. A worldly spirit having thus obtained a deep hold on the mind it is now necessary to consider how and by what means the society may be brought from under its influence and come to stand upon the original ground of love to God and to one another. If there is no alternative and we must go on as has been the case for more than fifty years it is almost a self-evident case that the society will in this way suffer itself to be robbed of the spiritual and heavenly standing it once held and the meetings for the worship of Almighty God be held in a very neglected manner. We may observe that during this decline there has been in almost all the settlements of Friends those who have been concerned to attend all their meetings and it is by the zeal and faithfulness of such that the society has been kept from falling away and losing their standing as a religious body. By taking a view of the concern of this class we shall find that from year to year they have had the maintenance of our religious meetings for worship much at heart and have given testimony in the extracts from their different Yearly Meetings expressive of the travail of the church on this important subject. Many of those valuable productions have been read in the meetings of Friends and then laid by to receive no further attention. If those testimonies of deep-felt concern were examined it has been thought that some of them at least might be rendered more useful by being spread before our young friends. They would in this way come to see the concern of society for their religious improvement. In the present state of the subject there seems but little to hope and much to apprehend; but though there is reason to be impressed with discouragement there is also some cause to believe Friends may be again revived and brought to feel our situation. If we were altogether a forsaken people we should find that the Lord answered no more either by vision or by prophecy. But this it is believed is not the case, because we find that our meetings are still at times clothed with a happy and precious solemnity and there are preserved among us those who are at times raised up to bear a living and reaching testimony. It therefore remains for Friends to try to keep a firm hold of the right thing, and try as way opens to stir one another up to love and good works. The neglected state of our religious meetings, particularly in or near the middle of the week should claim our care and attention. Let us endeavor to learn if possible what is the cause why members are so frequently absent and if it should be found on enquiry that some have embraced opinions opposed to the continuance of those meetings, if they cannot be convinced of their error, their cases should be introduced to the Monthly Meeting, and should they continue to oppose our meetings they should be disowned from the society. By this means if our number should be reduced for a time there is reason to believe that this would only be for a time, and as it would be manifest that those who remained in the society set a proper example and were themselves diligent attenders of our meeting, this would be encouraging to honest enquirers nor would it be long before we should find many applications to become members. There would be some encouragement to unite with a society that were alive in the fulfillment of their religious duty; but if we remain as we are in a state of weakness there can be no occasion for the seriously thoughtful to connect themselves with us. It is therefore necessary for Friends to come out of the present mixed and disorderly state, and short of this there is no reason to expect that the society will be improved and come to take the proper hold of the important Christian testimonies we have been called to maintain in the world.

ON THE FACULTY OF CONSCIENCE.—PART I.

I have lived in all good conscience before God unto this day—and again in this do I exercise myself daily to keep a conscience void of offence both towards God and man. Notwithstanding St. Paul maintained this high standing, it does not appear that he had received from his education, which was doubtless liberal, correct views of his religious duty—and therefore his conscience prior to his conversion must have been conformed to the opinions received from his preceptors. This is probably no uncommon case—but on the contrary quite general, and therefore it would not be proper to consider conscience an infallible guide. But as I have frequently heard it placed in that point of light, and believe that many hold this opinion of it, I have apprehended it might be useful to take up some inquiries upon the subject, and try, if possible, to show in what degree of credit this faculty should be held. As I have already mentioned, the conscience of St. Paul before his conversion must have been in agreement with the opinions of his preceptors. After his conversion, as his mind was altered, and as he now saw that he had been grossly in error, we are not to believe that this very great change was dictated by his conscience, consequently it must have been produced by the powerful operation of some other cause. By examining his own testimony upon the subject it will appear that he was convinced of his blindness by a supernatural light—by a light from Heaven—and being so convinced though the dictates of conscience were not changed, yet the points of conscientious approbation and disapprobation were. Formerly he was supposing he was doing God service by persecuting the disciples of Christ, and he had a conscience which did not condemn him for his zeal in this business. Now he finds by the interference of a supernatural principle that he was in the transgressing nature, and doing those things that were contrary to the divine mind. He is brought to this important discovery not by conscience, but by the light of Christ. From those facts it may be perceived that before man is humbled by the power of Truth, and brought to see himself in the light of Christ—that light which enlightens every man that comes into the world—his best guide is a fallible principle; a principle which can possess no more perfection in itself—than his judgment and as that has been formed in agreement with his education, he will conform to its rudiments. He will be a Jew, a Christian, or a Mahometan, and conscientiously regard the doctrines and opinions in which he has been educated. Darkness therefore will cover his mind, and it cannot be possible for him under those circumstances to have an infallible guide—because he is living in the transgressing nature, and is the subject of a state in which the mind and conscience are defiled. Hence to call upon those who are so circumstanced to obey their conscience is not fulfilling the duty of a gospel minister —nay it may even be the means of inviting such to transgress against God—conscience then in the unregenerate man is not a safe religious guide. It was not sufficient to awaken St. Paul and lead him out of error; nor is it a principle of any greater value in others—in the great concern of the soul's redemption. Before a conscience to be relied upon in the protection of the soul from defilement is formed—the individual must become subject to the divine visitation. He must be prostrated in a full conviction that he is a fallen and sinful creature—and that all his own acts, even his best acts are performed in conformity with a state of rebellion against God. After he has passed through this humbling view of himself and has come to see that he is undone without a Saviour—the foundation upon which he is engaged to build is changed. His mind obtains new views of itself—and those views being given by the presence of the light of Christ, a conscience is formed in him which is not built upon a human but upon a divine testimony. Now these are they that form the society of the multitude of believers who are of one heart and one soul—they consequently being led by an infallible guide out of darkness into the glorious light of the gospel, see eye to eye. And by keeping under the divine government, conscience in them compared to the light of the moon becomes as the light of the sun. Such witness great tenderness of spirit, and therefore enter deeply into the sufferings of Christ—they are wounded by every appearance of evil either in themselves or others. They all therefore "walk by the same rule and mind the same thing." In consequence of which they hold a united testimony, and are one in Christ. To them no duty is imposed by their own will or wisdom, but all is the immediate offspring of an infallible guide. If we go back into the history of these subjects of the kingdom of the Prince of Peace, we shall find that it never was the business of any of these to impose creeds and ceremonies upon the disciples of Christ. They have always aimed at maintaining obedience to the pure spirit, and contended that it is the letter that killeth, and the

Spirit only that giveth life. We are to look for the traditions of men and the imposition of rites and ceremonies from another class—and we shall find them among those of the Pharisaical order. There have been Pharisaical Jews and Pharisaical Christians—and the latter have been as numerous as the former. Through them there has been heaped upon the Christian profession a host of idolatrous duties, which are now contended for as conscientious obligations—and really are such upon the minds of those who are in the transgressing nature, and whom the Truth has never been permitted to set free. Those dark obligations of conscience have long tyrannized it over the children of God—and having set themselves up in the temple of God, they have assumed the prerogative of God,—and like Paul before his conversion, have supposed that in persecuting the true church they are doing God service. It therefore is important that the deceptions should be detected which have long been taking shelter under a supposed conscientious obligation, and which modern supposed Charity seems willing to credit as belonging to the heritage of God. But it would be as easy to unite light with darkness, or Christ with Belial, as to bring those idolatrous devotees with all their indulgence of a transgressing nature into this glorious abode of harmony and of Truth.

PART II.

After the foregoing observations it may be proper to show that a false conscience, or a conscience founded in delusion is as possible a case as a false or deluded judgment. When the advocates for the gospel of Jesus Christ who had been brought by the power of the Spirit of God out of darkness, engaged in the execution of their important mission, we do not find that they began their labors by taking hold of the learning and wisdom of man, nor did they lay it down as an essential in the Lord's work that men should become masters of the languages, or even that they should depend exclusively upon any outward means. On the contrary they came out with a plain testimony; they declared that all had sinned and fallen short of the glory of God—and therefore mankind were in bondage and held under chains of darkness. They proclaimed the necessity of repentance—that the old man with his deeds which are corruptible should be put off, and the new man put on—that the transgressing nature should be subdued, and a new and heavenly nature supply its place. Until this change was effected all was disorder—the mind and conscience defiled—and by no means prepared to judge in the great concerns of the church of Christ. But how does the case stand at present. Are we not informed of schools of divinity—theological students, fitting themselves up for the service of the church, and relying upon those endowments gained by study to prepare them to teach others the way in which they should go, while they are practically ignorant, and even enemies to the cross of the Redeemer. Walking in the pride and vanity of their own pompous imaginations, and daring to be judges of other men's consciences. Instead of themselves learning to be humble, and trusting to the shepherd of souls to instruct them and give them to see their blind and fallen state they are standing at a distance from the true ground, and as far as their influence extends keeping others also at a distance. From the commencement of those man-made ministers we may date the decline of vital christianity, and find substituted in its room the decrees of synods, and the dark and delusive doctrines of human wisdom supplying the place of the plain and precious precepts of the primitive ministers of Christ. Under those circumstances, the judgment is darkened, and of consequence, a conscience built upon it must be equally dark and ignorant. It is from those causes that the prosperity of the Messiah's kingdom is retarded.

ON DIVINE REVELATION.

It seems extraordinary, but is no less true, that while it is confessed there *has been* a revelation from God to man, it is denied that revelation is continued. Those who say so take up this conclusion, because they find the human family in the possession of ideas and opinions which they conceive could not have been obtained by the exercise of the natural senses alone, and because the scriptures of truth are a composition which so widely differ from all others, that they are almost necessarily admitted to be of supernatural origin. The question, therefore of a divine revelation being furnished at any time is a question of very great interest; because, if no such revelation has been furnished, then the scriptures should be rejected as an imposition upon the world. For every composition which is not what it professes to be, must of consequence be an imposition, and the greater the profession the greater the imposition. But the scriptures are a revelation from God to man, and therefore revelations have been. That they are a revelation may be proved from the doctrines they contain, being superior to all others,—from the events they have foretold coming literally to pass, and from their agreement with the convictions in every man's mind. The superiority of their doctrines is not denied by their most decided enemies. But this superiority could not be the effect of human sagacity;—for, if they had no higher fountain from whence to have proceeded, Scriptures or doctrines equally sublime might long since have become general. But if we examine the ideas and doctrines which have resulted from the natural talents of men, we shall find them to be in almost every point of view inferior. Hence we may surely conclude that the Scriptures are of supernatural origin; and consequently, that to those who wrote them a divine revelation was granted. The events foretold in them having literally taken place, is a fact which there is no difficulty in proving. Witness the unexampled destruction of Jerusalem,—the overthrow of the temple, and the remarkable dispersion of the Jews among all nations. Circumstances so critically fulfilled, that the prediction seems more like a history written after the events had taken place, than a prophecy preceding them.

In a calm deliberate attention to the important doctrines which the scriptures contain, no man can fail to have impressions furnished differing from those produced by the reading of any other book: and hence he must conclude that those impressions and convictions of their superiority are proofs of a supernatural origin.

If then we have clear evidence that divine revelations have been communicated to man,—surely we must admit that whatever has been may be again. Revelation has been and therefore may be again.

But what are the objections to a repetition of revelation? Can it be said that man is not the same now that he was when they were communicated? Is there any difference in the conformation of either his mind or body? Is the nature of moral obligations changed? Or are the passions and appetites altered? Will it be contended that the difficulty of such communications is rendered insuperable? Or can it be said that because a revelation has been given, that therefore all future communications from the Almighty would be useless? If we take the testimony of the scriptures on the subject, we shall find that they support a belief that revelation is to be expected as the common privilege of the faithful. 1 John, 2, 27, "But the anointing which ye have received of him abideth in you; and ye need not that any man teach you, but as the same anointing teacheth you of all things, and is truth and is no lie; and even as it hath taught you ye shall abide in him" Similar to this testimony is that delivered by Paul in his epistle to Titus, chap. 2, 11, 12, "For the grace of God that bringeth salvation hath appeared to all men teaching us, that denying ungodliness and worldly lusts, we should live soberly, righteously and godly in this present world." And again, 1 Corinthians, 12, 7, "But the manifestation of the spirit is given to every man to profit withal." I would ask, is it possible to understand those testimonies in any other light, or as having any other direct and plain meaning, than that of continued revelation?

By them we are told of a *principle* which "is truth, and is no lie;" and which is able to teach us all things; that this principle is the grace of God, and that it "hath appeared to all men,"—and the manifestation of the spirit which is given to every man to profit withal. Now if we are not to understand this spirit as having the power to reveal to us the will of God, and consequently, to teach us of all things necessary to our salvation, I can conceive no kind of useful meaning in them. But such was the meaning conveyed by the apostles; and therefore according to their testimonies revelation is continued to man.

Again, if we consider what it is that makes a difference between truth and falsehood, between light and darkness, as they alternately act upon us, I apprehend it will be impossible to explain this difference upon any other ground than that of the operation of the spirit which "searcheth all things, yea, the deep things of God." But take away this spirit, and let the human race be left to the mere powers of our natural intelligence, or to the operation of that knowledge which is acquired by sensation and reflection,—and let us examine what our qualifications would be under those circumstances. Sensation being outward, is manifestly excited by material objects, and reflections upon those objects, would be reflections upon natural and material things;—hence there would only be produced in us corresponding ideas;—and as those ideas would strictly agree with their exciting causes, of consequence there would be nothing spiritual in them. They would be the result of that natural sensation and reflection which constitutes the natural man who, according to Paul, "Receiveth not the things of the spirit of God, for they are foolishness unto him; neither can he know them because they are spiritually discerned." Which clearly implies, that the ideas of all things are only excited in us by their proper objects;—those that are natural by the presentation of natural and visible things and those that are spiritual by a divine and spiritual cause. If then the ideas of all things can only be excited by their corresponding objects, it must be evident, that while the knowledge of natural things is acquired by the presentation of natural objects to the natural senses,—those that are spiritual have a spiritual mode of presentation, and are only known in consequence of being presented to a spiritual capacity in man. Take away this capacity, and leave him wholly subject to natural sensation and reflection, and he could no more understand spiritual subjects,—than the natural man could understand sounds by sight or colors by hearing.

Hence we may surely conclude, that it has consisted with the order of perfect wisdom to constitute man both a natural and a spiritual being; and that those senses that are outward embrace the material and visible and the ideas thence arising pertain to the natural world. But, on the other hand, as he is not only a being of temporal and material existence, but also a being of spiritual and eternal duration, there are as well spiritual perceptions, as natural: and hence it is plain that those which are of the spiritual class are the perceptions which include the knowledge of divine and spiritual things. This appears to be the doctrine taught in the Holy Scriptures. They everywhere hold out the idea that God is a spirit—that man is made after his own image, and that temporal existence and objects belong to those capacities that are temporal—that those that are spiritual and eternal have capacities agreeing therewith—and that to these capacities are unfolded the revelations of the will of God. That by the exercise of them man is brought into a state capable of searching all things, yea, the deep things of God—and that through the medium of this spiritual capacity, every revelation of the divine will has been comprehended. But it may be said, these are assertions without proof—and therefore will not do to be relied upon. Is there any evidence that the human race ever did or ever can be certainly ascertained of anything but what comes under the cognizance of the five corporeal senses? To this we may reply that those who foretold future events which did certainly come to pass, must have been led to this knowledge by something different from the natural senses,—and this must have been a spiritual or divine intelligence.

As we pass along the important path of time circumstances take place which seem Providentially to remind us of the uncertainty of all visible things. In the case of Thomas Pim, late a respectable inhabitant of East Caln township, Chester county, this impression was made in a most powerful manner. He had left his family as usual, in his gig, in which he had been accustomed for many years to travel among his neighbors. The distance which he had contemplated going did not exceed a few miles; but finding after going a short distance that he was attacked with indisposition, he turned in order to reach home. It was however too late. Before he could again reach his habitation the vital spark had fled, and to an affectionate wife and family he was returned a corpse. The support which his wife in particular felt under the awful circumstance was admirable. It is not our intention on the present memorable occasion to say all that might be said, but it seems due in this case to mention some of the prominent features of the character of the deceased. He was one of those rare instances of a man who without much profession came up to the practice of doing as he would be done by. Among his neighbors he was social and free, and though he could plainly say to any man what he thought of him, he was seldom known to give offence. The writer of this memoir knew him well. In one instance they rode together to the house of a valuable acquaintance, where they arrived at an early hour of the morning. Our acquaintance said to T. P., "Thou art early at my house; I suppose thou art in pursuit of some worldly object, and if thou was as much in earnest about the kingdom of heaven as thou appears to be about the world's concern, thou would make no inconsiderable figure as a religious man." To which T. P. calmly replied, "that men were not to be taken by appearances—that he had long thought that there might be much show where there was but little substance, and that for his part he had rather never be known as a religious man than not come up to the duties which we owed to this world." In his family his manners were easy and pleasant, and his house was liberally opened to all his friends. Although he had been for many years much crippled by a complaint of the rheumatic character, and which made it difficult for him to move from one place to another, yet he was never heard to murmur; on the contrary, in the company of his friends he was cheerful and entertaining. To the poor who were the objects of his kindness, he was a warm and a useful friend. In their distress he aided them, and in their follies he reproved them. Plain and frank in his manners, few men did with more honesty speak their minds to their friends. Through life he was an example of moderation, and although industrious and attentive to his temporal concerns, he was never known to be oppressive. His tenants who took his advice were in common successful and uniformly respected him. By a regular system of economy and judicious management of his concerns he became wealthy; but in all his transactions he had the happiness to steer his course with so much caution that he was never known to have a law-suit on his own account. Within a short time before his death he seemed to be aware that his end was approaching; and with this view he was attentive to have nothing undone which rested on his mind to do. A few days before his departure he mentioned that he had but two visits to make, and if these were paid he should be done. It is believed he was in the act of paying this last one when he was called off. Having finished his course, we may justly say that as a husband, father, and friend, he was highly respected, and we have no doubt he will be much missed by many who knew and valued his company. It is a consolation in looking to his end to believe that though it was sudden he had nothing to do but to die.

In the organization of religious society it is necessary that the members should unite in the principle by which they are to be governed. If they believe in the fundamental obligations of Christianity, they will of course conclude that they are to be under and subject to that measure of the Spirit which the apostle Paul has said is given to every man to profit withal. By those who believe in this doctrine, it has been understood to be a Spirit that takes its kingdom by entreaty, and keeps it by humility, and a lowly or passive state of mind. Such a society must therefore be brought to place their whole confidence in the power and wisdom of this heavenly guide. They will under all circumstances confide in it, let their trials as individuals or as a society be what they may. They will never have recourse to any mode of relief but what they are convinced is dictated by this eternal Spirit. Now as the Society of Friends profess to have full faith in this divine gift, they are necessarily to submit themselves to it in all that they have to meet with in the world. It would be turning away from the principle of their profession if they should have recourse to any system of human policy in order to gain any point. The fact is, to a society that professes as Friends do, there is no door which can be opened to any other wisdom and power for the preservation of themselves or that of the order of the Society, but the wisdom and power of Truth. Now as it is understood that the Spirit they profess to embrace, acts not compulsively but by persuasion and a convincement of the judgment, so it is clear that its purposes are never to be gained by the arm of flesh. Hence we may infer that if the Society should from any cause be led away from a state of entire dependence upon this gift, it must be on the downward course, and consequently fail to maintain a true testimony to the excellency of their religious profession. In taking a view of the present circumstances of the professors of Christianity, there has appeared much reason to believe that many amongst them have been ready to conclude, since the Society of Friends have become a divided people, they have proved to the rest of mankind that it is not in the nature of their profession to keep them in connection or united together; and that from necessity they will have to abandon their confidence in the doctrine which they have professed, and come under the regulating power of fixed laws and rules of government. That the spiritual profession which they have held is incompatible with the nature of man, and that the party which they will prefer will be those who are called the "Orthodox" party: Because, say they, we can see in them something like an adoption of the doctrines and opinions of other religious professors. We are therefore placed under very serious circumstances, and it is highly necessary for Friends to endeavor clearly to understand the great responsibility that rests upon us; that so we may be found consistent with the fundamental principle of our profession. If we mean to take upon ourselves the same testimonies that were embraced and maintained by our worthy predecessors, it follows conclusively, that we must shut our eyes from the policy of the world, and turn away from any dependence upon the arm of flesh. We know that as to the past circumstances which we have witnessed, so far as they were distressing to many of us, they were the fruit of a departure from the true light that enlightens every man that comes into the world. Our early Friends having been convinced both of the power and wisdom of their heavenly guide, relied upon it in every trial; and being faithful to its manifestations, they became a body of people in perfect submission to the one eternal Spirit. In this happy state love reigned predominant among them, and hence they knew practically that as many as walked in this Light, as he the great author of it is light, had fellowship one with another. Now while Friends continued in this blessed state it was impossible for rents and divisions to take place. Hence they were an unconquerable body. But as they succeeded in convincing the world of their innocent lives and conduct, they were relieved from persecution, and soon became prosperous in the world. With the rise of character, and the increase of wealth, there was a gradual falling off from that state of watchfulness and devotion which had been maintained in the beginning; and from this cause men came to have an influence in the society, who had little more to recommend them than their wealth. Thus by a total change in the character and disposition of many of the leaders of Society, it followed that when difference of opinion arose on any subject, those high-minded individuals would not condescend to the views of their brethren. When therefore condescension was abandoned, strife succeeded; and a division was the consequence. But had the same spirit of brotherly regard been cherished which so eminently appeared among the founders of the Society, it would have been impossible for it to become divided. Our unhappy conflict and consequent separation must therefore not be charged to the profession, but to a want of individual faithfulness to the divine Spirit.

The same causes we must believe will produce the same effects: and therefore it is necessary for Friends to be on their guard, or otherwise strife and division may again take place. But in order to preserve the body from falling into this unhappy state, it is of vast importance that it should be grounded and settled in correct principles. On this subject the author has felt a deep concern. He is fully aware that at present we stand in a very critical situation, and he feels his fears lest there should be a want of just conceptions of the consequences which threaten to overtake us. He will therefore leave with his friends a testimony of his concern, and he believes it a duty to endeavor to call the attention of Friends to the alone ground of safety, and of prosperity to the great cause of universal peace and righteousness. It should never be forgotten by us that it is one thing to profess a belief in the Divine manifestation to man, and it is another thing to have a settled faith at all times and under all circumstances in the sufficiency of the wisdom and power of this gift. For want of this faith and patient awaiting the Lord's time, when trials and difficulties arise we may go to work in our own wisdom and strength in order to remove unpleasant cases when they occur. Thus by putting forth the hand unbidden to steady the ark we may bring death instead of life, and really retard the advancement of the good cause. It has been occasion of mourning to find that we are not so fully settled in the belief of the all-sufficiency of the precious gift as should be the case if Friends are not deeply attentive to the light and spirit of the great Head of the Church, they may introduce measures of human policy and be governed by them—the consequence of which must be that the society may again be landed much in the wilderness state. There was perhaps never a time when it was more important to the great cause of Christianity than the present time that all who profess with us should keep close to their proper places and duties, studying to show ourselves approved unto God. And as we believe that we live in an age when there is much enquiry in the minds of the people and when all the movements of those under our name are closely watched, much depends upon what we say and do in accordance with the witness for truth in the minds of enquirers. Our meetings for divine worship being held as they are with a profession of waiting in spirit upon the great Head of the Church to be instructed by him, it has appeared clear to me that if Friends were deep and weighty in their spirits they would be more often favored with the overshadowings of Divine love and thereby be refreshed together, as well as witness the power of truth to be raised into dominion; and thus, forward spirits that come among us, and often wound the spiritual life by running into words without life and power would be kept down. There is perhaps no circumstance which has a greater tendency to mar the work of righteousness in the earth than a lifeless ministry. Some there are who with a small gift would be favored to know the burden of the word given to them, and would be clear in what they had to deliver, but for want of keeping in the littleness, and by giving way to the desire to enlarge, are clouded in their testimony and judgment, and do not furnish anything like a certain sound, or learn .to know their proper stopping places. Hence they remain in the mixture, and Friends are often at a loss to know whether there is a gift or not: and when some of these are at last from their weak appearances advised to desist and try to keep silent, they become troublesome to Friends.

Leaving the subject of the Ministry, it remains with me to remark, that in order to maintain the testimonies of truth on the true ground, there is no point more important than that of a strict regard to the peaceable nature of the gospel spirit. So long as we trust to any other means than that of the Divine Gift for the safety and well-being of the society, we shall be liable to weakness and error: but if we place our confidence exclusively in the Divine Gift and follow it, there will be nothing to fear. But it is to be feared that many among us are not in possession of the true and living faith,—a faith that overcometh the world. The society of Friends from their rise have been firmly of the judgment that the light of Christ inwardly manifested is the alone sure guide, and by it every individual may be instructed in all the subjects that pertain to the Kingdom of Heaven. They have therefore maintained this testimony, that with them it is the first and primary rule of faith and practice. We make the same profession, and therefore have no new doctrine to preach; but the same that has been from the beginning, and which is preached in every creature. In this we are different from other professors of Christianity, who consider that revelation has ceased, because (say they) God has committed his will to writing. If this doctrine was true, it would follow as a consequence that none could be saved but those who could read, and who had the book. We do not advert to this doctrine with any view to controversy, but simply to present a correct view of the profession of Friends from the beginning. Now as we have embraced the doctrine of a Divine manifestation to man, and do not believe that in this blessed gift there is any tendency to strife or contention, or that it is incompetent to the preservation of those individuals, or that society which live in subjection to its teachings—it is of great importance to us and to the cause of Truth, that we should in our practice conform to it. It never can be right for a people making this high profession, to have recourse to compulsory measures in defence of themselves or of the order of the society. On the contrary, when they are brought under trials and difficulties, they should manifest their full faith in the gift. Thus they would be qualified to stop the mouths of gainsayers and all that should rise up against them. When a body of men are united in any one profession it is the duty of the individual members of that body to adopt the doctrine they have embraced. Hence it follows that as the Society of Friends wholly abandon all that kind of management which belongs to the children of this world, and to its policy,—they have only to trust to the pure and heavenly gift; and surely they have every reason to do so. When we look back into the trials and sufferings which our dear friends had to encounter, and observe with what meekness, patience, and fortitude, they endured those impositions,—looking to the Lord alone for deliverance—surely we might be both encouraged and instructed to trust to the same blessed power for deliverance from the comparatively insignificant difficulties of our time. It is of great importance to the society of Friends that they should not only understand the fundamental principle of their profession, but that they should have full faith in the power and virtue of it: and having the example of our early Friends before us and finding from their case that they were happily sustained under all trials in consequence of their obedience to the principle of their profession we are left without excuse should we attempt to take any other ground or seek a deliverance from trials by the aid of the arm of flesh or the policy of the world. The whole power of the church of Christ is centered in love. Therefore in all cases where there is opposition, it is the business of the true believer to try to overcome by maintaining a meek and gentle spirit. But should any attempt to subdue and regulate disorderly spirits by the exercise of compulsory measures, they would only mar the work and wound themselves. From the commencement of the society, we may see that all the extreme cases, such as have ended with rendings and division, have been produced by a departure from the spirit of meekness, forbearance, and brotherly kindness. And we may always depend upon it, that if we cannot gain the desired point by the exercise of those Christian principles, that we should not resort to any other. The fact is if we do in any degree depart from the true ground, we may be sure of losing by it.

In reflecting upon the doctrine of rewards and punishments, it has presented as a clear case that it never was consistent with the attributes of the Deity to impose suffering upon any of his creatures. But he has done all that could be done to make all parts of his creation happy; and therefore all the misery that we experience is the consequence of our own misconduct. In the formation of man it appears that it was consistent with the wisdom of his great Author to constitute him a being capable of devotion; and to this end he gave to him an amount of freedom agreeing with the capacity that he was endued with. Hence he would think for himself, and make his own elections by following his passions and appetites, and indulging them, he would run into excesses, and those excesses would produce their own sufferings. Experience teaches us that every act has its consequence. Thus we find a motive for self-government, and as we learn on the one hand that every improper indulgence produces misery, so we find on the other that the more we become subject to the principle of self-government, the greater is our happiness. In those two cases of fact we have full proof that it is not the pleasure of the Creator that we should be sufferers, but that he has done all that could be done consistent with the nature of our being to render us completely happy. Had we been created without any portion of freedom, we could never have known or enjoyed devotional feelings, but must have moved along in life as mere machines. Having then a devotional capacity, it must follow that when all our experience proves the goodness of God to us in giving us the means of happiness, that this knowledge should excite the highest sense of obligation, and of course the most pure devotion and love to God. If we were obliged to contemplate him in any other light, it would have the most melancholy effect upon us.

Finding, then, that by regarding the light of Truth and walking in it, we give energy and dominion to our more exalted and higher nature, and witnessing daily the consequence to be a complete quietude of the passions, and the most perfect possession of intellectual happiness, we are thus united to the great Fountain of spiritual good, and are one with our glorious author. We cannot believe, while possessing this blessed state, that it ever was any part of the design or purpose of God to render any part of his creation miserable. Of course we must be convinced that all the miseries of mankind are the fruit of their own doings. According to those views it will appear that there is nothing in the attributes of God that ever can consist with dealing out penalties and afflictions upon his finite creatures. Hence we come to the belief that because it was necessary in order to our own preservation, that evil and folly should bring sufferings upon us as a consequence, or otherwise we should never be brought out of it; therefore those sufferings themselves are demonstrations of the goodness and mercy of God to man. The truth appears to be that in every case where we witness suffering, there is no more of it than seems necessary to promote their own good. In looking into the human composition, and considering it in agreement with the foregoing sentiments, we find an admirable proof of the sublimity and greatness of the christian system. By this we are taught to believe that we have to control all our animal passions, in order to become acceptable to God; and by our own positive practical knowledge we are convinced that our happiness can never be completed by sensual indulgences. The obligations of christianity and those that are found from the operation of the laws of our nature, both prove that they have the same origin; that is, the wisdom that dictated the christian's path of duty, and that fixed the consequences of sensual excess is one and the same. Therefore, however the reputed philosopher, or the common sceptic may point the finger of derision at the humble and self-denying follower of the Son of God, it is impossible for himself to be happy in any other course of life than that which is adopted by the latter. But we are told that there must be some mistake on the part of those who would prohibit the indulgence of the passions and appetites of nature. Why, say they, were they given, if they must be kept in such strict subordination? The answer is not difficult, because it is easy to prove that the same wisdom and power that gave those dispositions, has set for them the requisite boundary, and no man can pass it without bringing upon himself consequences of a suffering kind. From which we might expect every enlightened individual would surely be convinced that the precepts themselves that are taught by Christianity have flowed from the same fountain of perfect wisdom.

RESPECTED FRIEND:

As by thy letter I am informed of the interest thou hast felt in the subject which has been lately agitated in your meeting—it has appeared to me that I might state in answer—that as to the subject itself there appears in my mind no difficulty—but I feel some concern lest my friends should too zealously dispute upon it—the foundation upon which society must stand, if it stands at all, is the spirit of condescension and mutual forbearance—any degree of selfishness or opposition must be destructive of its very existence so far as it is permitted to take hold. On this general principle I have ever thought it safe to give my judgment to my friends—and having done so passively to leave the subject—thou seest therefore that as it relates to any question which may be agitated among Friends I can have no point to carry—my judgment being settled that all conclusions which take place in the harmony are right as respect the body which adopts them though they may be defective as respects the question settled. In the order of society there is a necessary subordination to be observed, and without which confusion must follow. No question can be finally settled by a Monthly Meeting which does not come within the limits of its province, and all questions which relate to general practice must of consequence be settled by general consent. The general practice of society in regard to marriage can never be settled by a Monthly Meeting, but must be guided by the harmonious conclusion of the Yearly Meeting. Let it be supposed that with a small exception in your Monthly Meeting, the society are uniform in the marriage covenant—and enter into that solemn obligation by the same form of expression. Canst thou conceive that such uniformity should be changed in a society professing to be led by the one spirit and formed into the one body especially where the act is the same, as is the fact in the case of marriage? If every Monthly Meeting within the limits of our Yearly Meeting were to take up the question and deviate in the same degree from each other that Sadsbury appears to have done, what would be the consequence? Would it not produce very disagreeable impressions—and that they would be liable to deviate cannot be doubted by any one who is acquainted with the present state of society—I therefore conclude that subjects of a general kind are wisely held within the control of the Yearly Meeting—therefore without entering into the arguments which might be used on either side of the subject—I hold it safe for me to stand subordinate to the present custom of the society—but should the objections rise in any to the present custom so high as that they might believe it proper to lay them before a Monthly Meeting, and thence to take their regular course to a quarterly, and so if found of sufficient weight, to a Yearly Meeting. In that stage I should be willing to try the whole subject—at present I do not consider it open for discussion, and shall consequently avoid any specific sentiment upon it. I am satisfied with what has been the uniform practice of society—and willing to remain so until the subject in the course of order and in the line of my duty shall come before me. If from what I have said thou should be in any manner benefited, thou art welcome to so much of the attention of thy affectionate friend,

JESSE KERSEY.

ON THE DIVINITY OF CHRIST.

On recurring to the feelings which I have often had by hearing the divinity of Christ spoken of, it has at length seemed to me that it would be right to put some of my thoughts on this subject on paper. I shall therefore complete this design in as plain a manner as I am capable of. In the first place, I shall state that I cannot credit any doctrine that implies a plurality of gods, and therefore I am persuaded that throughout the Scriptures wherever a divine influence or operation is spoken of, it must always relate to the great all-powerful, all-wise, and first Cause. And he is unlimited in his nature, and must be in all things, so all the effects produced either in the mental or physical world are effects produced by the one eternal great first Cause. Hence I conclude that when Paul speaks of the Son of God, and declares him to be the Wisdom and Power of God, the same by which the worlds were made, he means neither more nor less than this: that the Wisdom and Power of God when they become active, as must have been the case in the formation and production of this visible creation, they must be viewed as effects of God, and in that sense they proceed from him, and hence he calls the Wisdom and Power of God the Son. In the same sense I can only understand the Evangelist John, where he has said "in the beginning was the Word, and the Word was with God, and the Word was God; all things were made by him, &c." That is agreeing with Paul, "in the beginning was the Wisdom and Power of God, and the Wisdom and Power was with God, and was God. All things were made by this Wisdom and Power." This Wisdom and Power is then the beginning of the creation of God, and in that sense alone being an effect of God, is the Son. Now in whatever way the great first cause may manifest himself, that manifestation is an effect of God, and therefore the Son. Every manifestation which it has pleased God to make of himself is an effect of God. Such was the case when his Wisdom and Power appeared in the person of the man Jesus. His body was not the divinity for it was a finite body; it was capable of animal life and death. It was the Wisdom and the Power that was manifest through that body that was the true divinity. Now as God is one eternal, all-wise, undivided, and unchangeable being, so God was manifest in the flesh, and he is manifest in the flesh in all his saints. They are one as God is one, and while they remain in God they must be one and undivided. The great clamor that has been raised in the Society about denying the divinity of Christ, and which made its appearance in England in the treatment of Hannah Barnard, is much of it the fruit of the same spirit that appeared in the defence of the absurd doctrine of the Trinity; and this doctrine of three distinct divisions of the great first Cause has always been the cause of producing absurd opinions and divisions among men from its commencement. Among the professed Jews they had nothing like it; nor does it appear from anything said by Jesus himself that he wished for any such divided views to be entertained. I and my Father, says he, are one. Now let the manifestations or operations of the Eternal be when they may, or what they may, they are from himself and therefore they are and can be but one. All the notions that are held about Father, Son, and Holy Ghost appear therefore without any rational foundation. The fact is, God is one and undivided, and if when we speak of an operation of God upon the soul of man, we were governed by this undivided view of the divine nature, there would be less mystery in the doctrines delivered than is now the case. In the formation of man he is acknowledged to be the work of God, and in his government and perfect regulation it is an effect that must result from the influence of the one eternal spirit of God. If then in the ministry of the gospel it were the practice to show that in all cases where transgression takes place it is the one eternal Spirit that is opposed by our evil acts, and that to this pure and perfect principle we must be united before we can be happy, the nature of man's redemption and salvation would be better understood than is the case under the generally received opinions.

It is evident from some of the productions of latter time that the Society of Friends, who came out from under the dominion of formal professors of religion and manifested that they had been visited and enlightened by the one great and good God, and therefore attained to the possession of clear spiritual views of the nature of the Christian religion and the spirituality of its character, have returned to the beggarly elements, and really seem determined again to renew those formal bonds from which we had been in some measure made free. We have the evidence of this from the material or corporeal ideas they seem now to entertain of the Saviour of men. Holding up to one another the material blood that was shed on Calvary's mount, and thereby justifying the Jews in the murder of the man Jesus—for the divinity they could not slay. Our friends in the beginning had some just conception of the one only wise God our Saviour, and could by no means agree to a plurality of gods; and if the Society would follow the leadings of this pure fountain of perfection, their understandings would become clear in the things of God. They would clearly discover that the whole work of religion was spiritual and not carnal.

ON THE DOCTRINE OF FATHER AND SON.

Having from my childhood been much puzzled with what I believed to be the doctrine of Christianity on the subject of the Father and Son, I shall here state some of the difficulties into which this doctrine frequently led me, and attempt to explain the whole subject in conclusion upon principles which may be comprehended and understood. And first as to the difficulties:—I could not comprehend how it should be possible that three beings should be one being. Every thing that was to be found in the world stood distinct, and no proposition is more clear than the following,—that no two things can at the same time be one thing. But the doctrine imposed by the advocates of Christianity requires us to believe that God, the Father, is one thing, and that God, the Son, is another, and that those two are one. If we do not believe this we cannot be Christians—and if we do believe it we must believe it in contradiction to reason, and to the evidence of every thing around us. This would be a belief founded in ignorance, and consequently a prostration of the faculties received from that God who it is said has imposed upon us this difficulty. The disputes of professed divines have been almost endless upon this subject—and their contrary arguments are only calculated to involve the honest enquirer in deeper perplexity. Schoolmen have personified the Trinity, and added to their many absurd propositions the additional difficulty arising from the opinion that those three Persons are after all to be acknowledged as one Person. Were a philosopher to tell us that the sun, the moon, and the earth are one—he would have as full a claim to our belief of this sentiment upon the plain principles of the human understanding, as those divines who assert that there are three persons in the Godhead. Man is a being, it is true, of limited capacity; and it would be expecting too much of him that he should fully comprehend all the mysteries of God and nature. It would be equally absurd that he should refuse his assent to the truth of fundamental principles, because he did not fully comprehend them. There are principles which though they may be above his reason, yet do not contradict it, and in which it is proper for him to have faith, however impenetrable they may be to his understanding. Such is the first principle of all religion, the being of a God—that anything should exist without a cause, and that anything should be the cause of its own existence, are propositions that exceed our reason. We are utterly incapable of penetrating this secret, and yet we must believe that one of them is true or nothing could ever have existed. We see therefore that it is not for us to understand all the principles by which the universe is governed. But if a statement is made of principles contradictory to our reason, here we have a right to doubt, and cannot be required to give our assent—such for instance, as that two things can at the same time be one. Happy for the cause of Christianity, it involves no such absurd requisitions. It is plain in its principles and easily comprehended. With this view I shall confine myself to the testimonies of the scriptures, and show that they contain no personal doctrines on the question. The evangelist John has said that "in the beginning was the word, and the word was with God, and the word was God. All things were made by him, and without him there was not any thing made that was made." By this testimony we are informed that God created all things; and it clearly conveys the idea, that the Almighty and his creative power operating to the production of all things, are as cause and effect. That is, that the Creator was entire, having in himself the fullness of all existence; and therefore his will to create must be subsequent to that of his power and wisdom. But when he determined upon creation, his wisdom, his power, and will to create, came into action. The moment, therefore, in which creative power began to operate, an effect proceeded from himself: and as it was God, so it was also an effect of God, and therefore one with him. In this sense the creative power of God is spoken of in the revelations;—where the Son is said to be the beginning of the creation of God; and Paul mentions that by him the worlds were made—consequently the power and wisdom of God when it came into action in the production of a universe, is an effect of God, and in this sense is clearly the offspring of God. But though it is the offspring of God, it is nevertheless in the nature of God, and cannot be separated from him. In this view of the doctrine of Father and Son we have a most happy conviction of the simplicity of another testimony of the scriptures, where it is said that God was in Christ, reconciling the world unto himself. This implies that the same creative power which was in the beginning and by which the worlds were made, is still operating for the restoration of man. That is to say that the perfect man can only be formed now as at the first by the all-creative power of God. Viewing therefore the doctrine of Father and Son as containing the idea in a qualified sense of cause and effect, we are by this conclusion entirely freed from the absurd opinions which enjoin the belief that two beings are one. Nor do I find from a rational construction of the testimonies concerning God and Christ which the scriptures contain, any evidence to contradict or oppose the foregoing construction—from the time in which Jesus Christ began his ministry until his ascension, we find the constant dependence upon his Father acknowledged,—and we have the same proof that he always maintained that he and his Father were one, that his outward manifestation in the flesh was an effect of the all-creative power will not be denied. This was manifest in the testimony delivered by the angel to Mary, when he said to her, "Fear not, Mary, for thou hast found favor with God; and thou shalt conceive and bring forth a son and shall call his name Jesus." But Mary adverting to the common course in nature, could not reconcile this testimony with her knowledge of facts: and when she doubted, she was informed that the Holy Ghost should come upon her and the power of the Highest should overshadow her. Consequently the creative power and offspring of God was manifest in the birth of Christ.

DEAR HANNAH:

IN writing thee this letter, I am under the feelings of a father, and attended with the recollection that I am addressing an only and last remain of a very interesting company of eleven children. Thou may very reasonably believe when thou reflects upon my time of life, that I consider this communication as one of the last demonstrations of parental regard and love for thee. I shall therefore write in perfect agreement with the feelings of my heart. In the first place, I will remark that much of thy time so far in life has been spent under trials and real afflictions. But remember that troubles arise not out of the dust, nor do troubles and afflictions come out of the ground. Thou may charge them to causes that have been out of thy control; but remember that this is not the case throughout, and so far as any of them may be chargeable to thyself, learn I entreat thee by the things thou hast suffered. The disposition to charge others is nothing new in the world. It began early with the human race, and has continued ever since, and it is the way by which many seem to expect an acquittal from all their faults. But I would advise thee, as an experienced father, not to take this course, but let all thy troubles be charged to their just causes, and this will be the best way to get rid of them properly or to overcome them. In discharging our duty faithfully there is always a happy reward; and hence it was said, say ye to the righteous it shall go well with him, for the reward of his hands shall be given; but say ye to the wicked that it shall go ill with him, for he shall receive the fruit of his own doings. So that the fact is that all our doings receive their own reward, whether they be good or evil. As thou must be aware of this fact, I here close all remarks of this kind. And now, Hannah, I wish thee to understand that I have no confidence in that kind of passage through life that leans upon public acts of charity. To be a christian and really to enjoy the evidence of divine favor we must remember that they that become the disciples of Jesus Christ lead a life of self-denial, and take up the cross daily. This is the doctrine that we profess; this sublime doctrine, ah how it would ornament the Society if it were constantly in practice. Every passion in nature in that case would be subdued; all pride and self-importance would be conquered, and we should be known by all our conduct and conversation to be the followers of the blessed Jesus. Our hearts would be clothed with the covering of humility, and that love of one another which would demonstrate that we had passed from death to life.

DEAR HANNAH:

THY letter of the 7th instant has come to hand, and were it not that I am desirous of satisfying an inquiring mind on a doctrinal subject I believe that I should not have attempted to write in return so soon. The fact is, that it is more of a task to me to write now than formerly. But reflecting upon the subject offered to my consideration by thy young friend, it has occurred to me that the best expounder of the doctrines of Christ is the light of his own blessed Spirit in every mind. But there may be instances of individual cases where instrumental helps are right and proper. In all such I doubt not but the instrument will be called to the case when the right time shall come. Upon the doctrine itself I am free to say that the word atonement does not very happily apply to the subject, because the word reconciliation is more in accordance with the condition called for, and which is the great end of the gifts of divine Providence to man. Now it is our sins that separate us from the one true and living God, and we never can be united to him until we are separated from transgression. As many as are led by the Spirit of God, they are reconciled unto him and are his sons. But those who have taken up the doctrine that the sins of mankind are atoned for by one great offering appear to me to have adopted a mass of absurd opinions, and attributed to the great Parent of mankind dispositions, and even a character that never did belong to him. They charge the whole human family with having committed crimes against the great attribute of justice which can never be forgiven until there is a satisfactory atonement made for all those offences. Thus they assume a character to the divine Being which never belonged to him. They have even held up the idea that he is absolutely inexorable, and stands off from us in a state of high displeasure. But his Son, compassionating our case comes forward and offers to take charge of our case. He therefore to satisfy the inexorable Father comes to our world, and so plans the whole concern that some of those very creatures who were the objects of his concern put him to the ignominious death of the cross, and by this act we are put into the capacity to have our sins atoned for, and we are put into a capacity to be saved. In order to be a firm believer in the doctrine of the atonement, upon orthodox principles, we must admit the existence of a plurality in the divinity. We must have the being making the atonement, and also the being to whom it is made. Christianity never held up this kind of belief to the world. The Evangelist John is perfectly clear on the subject, and plainly proves that in the beginning was the Word, and the Word was with God, and the Word was God. Now the apostle Paul has clearly shown that the Word spoken of by the Evangelist John is the wisdom and power of God, the same by which the world was made, and confirms the whole doctrine of Christianity to centre the believer in the belief that though in the world there are lords many and gods many, to the Christian there is but one God. The whole, therefore, of the doctrine of Father and Son is clearly shown to consist of cause and effect. Viewing the subject in this light, it must forever put an end to the dark doctrine of the atonement as believed in or professed by the orthodox believer. For many years I have not been able to believe in the doctrine of a plurality in the divine character, and hence I have seen as Paul expresses himself upon the subject that to us there is but one God. Now in regard to Jesus of Nazareth, born of the virgin Mary, there has been no difficulty to my mind in believing that if it consisted with the wisdom of God to cause a virgin to conceive and bring forth a son, his power was sufficient to accomplish the design, and Jesus being so brought forth might very properly be called, as he really was, the Son of God. But though he may be thus spoken of and understood, still I have to believe that when at any time he performed a marvellous act, such as opening the eyes of the blind, causing the lame to walk, or the dead to be raised, this was done by the power of God and not by Jesus as a man. Now it is from this understanding in regard to Jesus of Nazareth, born as aforesaid, that my mind is relieved from all those dark and absurd opinions that embrace Jesus as a second person in the Trinitarian system. I know and I can know but one God, and because the light which shines in me and in all men is an effect of God, it is therefore called the Son of God Christ within the hope of glory. Nor is there any other means or medium by which we can be led to the knowledge of God but by this same Christ, within whom is the true light that enlighteneth every man that cometh into the world. We know in the outward, that it is, by the rays of light that proceed from the sun that we are led up to a knowledge of the sun. In like manner is the mind by the Spirit led up to the knowledge of God.

Having had my understanding thus opened and informed upon those important points, I have entered seriously into the consideration of the mediation offered by this heavenly light in us and I have seen that all those who in obedience to his invitation, come unto him and take his yoke upon them do enter into his gentle and lamb-like nature. Thus they cease to do evil and learn to do well and hence it is that there is nothing in them that would hurt or destroy, and therefore they are one with the Eternal united in him. But let us look a little further into the doctrine that supposes Christ died as an atonement for the sins of mankind, and see what is said that may fairly apply to the subject. We find the first Christian martyr Stephen, speaks to the Jews of that time and it is probable there were some of the persons who heard this servant of God had been parties in the murderous act which he charged upon them, when he had so clearly set before them the goodness of God to them and their forefathers. And in return how had they and their forefathers acted. O ye stiff-necked and uncircumcised in heart and in ears. Ye do always resist the Holy Ghost, as your fathers did, so do ye. Which of the prophets have they not slain? and lastly ye have with wicked hands murdered the just one. I ask with what propriety could Stephen have considered this act of the crucifixion of the Son of God as being done in violent opposition to the requirings of the Divine Spirit, if it be true that it was necessary to be done for the redemption of the world. No, the fact is, if the attributes of the Divine Being ever recognized measures of a cruel nature for the redemption of a fallen world, then I have through life been kept from understanding the subject rightly and must have been deceived. But it may be further remarked that Jesus himself said at a certain time, "And now O, Father I have glorified thee on earth, and I have finished the work which thou gavest me to do." As this testimony concerning himself was before his crucifixion, it is evident that what followed his testimony was the work of men and therefore not necessary to be done. It may be proper to add that those who think that the outward death and sufferings of Christ were necessary to satisfy the great attribute of justice certainly, in looking for this suffering as a remedy for the sins of the world, require in concurrence with their belief one of the greatest acts of injustice that can be conceived, to do away the effect of injustice. The truth of the matter is that in relying upon the outward crucifixion for salvation, they appear to go from all that is just or reasonable and to require us to believe a doctrine which goes farther to tolerate rapine, cruelty and death, than any other we have ever seen or heard of. No marvel that it was entirely exploded by our early Friends.

I now forward this letter which has been some time in my desk and not taken notice of. Perhaps it may serve to show thee that thou hast more place in the thoughts of thy Father than thou wast aware of.

JESSE KERSEY.

12th mo. 26th, 1840.

www.ingramcontent.com/pod-product-compliance
Lightning Source LLC
LaVergne TN
LVHW010218110826
845151LV00004B/1124
* 9 7 8 1 4 2 5 5 2 7 0 9 9 *